Spelling
Teacher's Resource Book

Carol Matchett

Schofield&Sims

Free downloads available from the Schofield & Sims website

A selection of free downloads are available from the **Spelling** page of the Schofield & Sims website (www.schofieldandsims.co.uk). These may be used to further enhance the effectiveness of **Schofield & Sims Spelling**. The downloads, which are kept updated as necessary to meet the requirements of the National Curriculum, add to the range of print materials supplied in the **Teacher's Guide** and **Teacher's Resource Book**. They include the following items:

- **National Curriculum correlation charts** show you exactly where each National Curriculum requirement for spelling is covered in the **Schofield & Sims Spelling** pupil books. Page numbers are provided for reference to the relevant activities. Where appropriate, notes from the non-statutory rules and guidelines are included.

- **Supplementary spelling logs** reinforce the words from the statutory word lists in the National Curriculum. Accompanied by a brief **User's guide**, the lists reflect the order in which the words are introduced in the **Schofield & Sims Spelling** books and can be used to encourage pupils to monitor their own spelling of these words – for example, using one list each half term.

- **Tricky words extra** (for Years 1 and 2) lists examples of common words that are exceptions in some accents but not others.

- A further **My tricky words** sheet enables you and your pupils to make tricky words lists of your own.

- An **Alternative spellings** document gives examples of words that have more than one correct spelling.

Please note: Throughout the **Spelling** series, sounds are shown in inverted commas and spellings in bold: for example, the 'oi' sound and the **oy** spelling.

First published in 2013

Copyright © Schofield & Sims Limited 2013

Author: **Carol Matchett**

Carol Matchett has asserted her moral right under the Copyright, Designs and Patents Act, 1988, to be identified as the author of this work.

British Library Catalogue in Publication Data:

A catalogue record for this book is available from the British Library.

Commissioned by **Carolyn Richardson Publishing Services (www.publiserve.co.uk)**

Design by **Oxford Designers & Illustrators**

Printed in the UK by **Page Bros (Norwich) Limited**

ISBN 978 07217 1219 2

Contents

Introduction

Schofield & Sims Spelling

This Teacher's Resource Book is part of the **Schofield & Sims Spelling** programme. This is a structured whole-school scheme designed to develop pupils' spelling skills and knowledge – both systematically and progressively. The programme follows the teach → practise → apply → assess model (see pages 6–10 of the **Teacher's Guide**) and consists of:

● six **pupil books** containing activities that will help pupils learn rules, strategies, patterns and guidelines so that they become accurate and confident spellers

● a **Teacher's Guide**, which helps you plan, teach and assess spelling; detailed teaching notes provide practical suggestions for how to introduce each page of the pupil books

● this **Teacher's Resource Book**, which provides photocopiable material to support the teaching, learning and assessment of spelling; you will find references within the Teacher's Guide to the resources found in this book.

Six **pupil books**

Teacher's Guide: teaching notes for all six pupil books

Teacher's Resource Book:
● extension and revision copymasters
● reminders and prompts
● assessment resources

The Teacher's Resource Book

The resources within this book are divided into two parts, as follows.

Part one: Resources to support teaching and learning

These copymasters support teaching and learning and can be used in the 'teach', 'practise' and 'apply' stages for revision or extension work. Some of them are specifically designed to follow up a page in the pupil book; you will find references to these activities within the 'Teaching notes' section of the **Teacher's Guide**. Others are more general resources that can be used at your discretion.

Part two: Assessment and record-keeping resources

These materials support the 'assess' stage with ongoing weekly and periodic assessment of spelling. Again, some of the copymasters are generic, while others are designed to be used at specific stages: for example, at the end of a section in the pupil book.

Part one:
Resources to support teaching and learning

1 Introduction to Part one

In this part of the book you will find the following materials for classroom use to support the 'teach', 'practise' and 'apply' stages:

- extension and revision activities
- reminders and prompts.

2 Using the extension and revision activities

These copymasters can be used at your discretion, to reinforce or extend the learning points from the pupil books.

They can be used for:

- additional group or individual activities that will extend or reinforce the spelling rules, patterns and guidelines introduced earlier
- introducing a focus to the class or group in a different way from that described in the **Teacher's Guide**.

For example, during the week a particular focus is introduced, a copymaster activity could be used to extend more able pupils by setting up an investigation or applying a guideline to other words. In subsequent weeks, an activity might be used to revise or reinforce a guideline or rule: for example, it might introduce the word in a different way or using a different context.

The extension and revision copymasters include the following items.

Additional word lists

These feature more words that follow the same rule, guideline or pattern as those in the pupil book. They can be used to investigate patterns further or to give more practice in applying rules and guidelines.

The lists can be photocopied and given to pupils for them to study and learn. For example, you could ask them to use coloured pencils or markers to emphasise the patterns. The lists can also be used in partner games such as 'Partner challenge', 'Find a friend' or 'Describe the word' (details of which are included on page 17 of the **Teacher's Guide**), or used in conjunction with the 'Word sort' copymasters described below to create an investigative activity.

Spelling logs

'Spelling log 1' folds up to make a small booklet that pupils can keep with them when writing. Pupils select words they think will be useful when writing. These could be words from the pupil book for reinforcement, or additional words relating to the focus: for example, words with suffixes. 'Spelling log 1' has space for five words at a time, so might be used with younger children or for words related to a particular piece of writing. 'Spelling log 2' has space for 12 words at a time. Pupils tick the words in their personal log each time they are used successfully in their writing. This activity can also encourage pupils to use more adventurous words in their writing.

Word sort copymasters

These can be used in conjunction with other resources (such as 'Additional word lists', 'Word collector' copymasters or words from the pupil book) to investigate or reinforce rules and spelling patterns. For example, pupils may be asked to sort words according to their spelling of a vowel phoneme or according to the rule applied to add a suffix.

You can give pupils a blank copy of the copymaster for them to decide on suitable column headings. Alternatively, you can make one copy and add the appropriate column headings before making copies to give to the pupils. There are three versions available, to allow words to be sorted by two, three or four criteria.

Word collector copymasters

These are designed for pupils to collect words with a particular spelling pattern. Two versions are provided for variety. Pupils are asked to search for words in a text or dictionary, or to collect them over a period of time from their reading. The words can be learnt or used in a word-sort activity.

Words to practise: Spelling practice ladders

This reinforcement copymaster is designed for individual practice of words that need special attention. These might be words that are spelt wrongly in the weekly dictation, or words pupils consistently get wrong in independent writing. The word is written correctly and then practised by saying and writing it a number of times.

3 Using the reminders and prompts

Ensuring that pupils apply in their independent writing what they have learnt in spelling sessions can be a challenge. The 'Target reminders' and 'prompt-style' copymasters are designed to help pupils remember spelling strategies, key learning points and routines when they are writing. All these points should be discussed with the class and the routines and strategies modelled so they become established as basic classroom practice. Copies of the prompts and reminders can then be displayed in the classroom, given to the pupils or stuck in spelling journals and exercise books for pupils to use at appropriate times.

The reminders and prompts include the following items.

Target reminders

These are designed to record spelling targets and then to keep them visible and in the pupils' minds while they are writing. There are separate fold-over and placemat versions. For examples of targets see page 48. There is also a mini-target version to remind children about specific tricky or topic words.

Words to practise: Tricky words and topic words

These are blank versions of the 'Tricky word' logs and 'Topic word' logs found in the pupil books, for handing out to your class, to groups or to individuals. You can use them to create lists of words relating to current topics or lists of particularly troublesome words. As pupils learn to monitor their own spelling, they can use a blank sheet to create their own personal lists.

Learning and practising tricky words

These copymasters give pupils a summary of the strategies they have learnt to help them spell tricky high-frequency words, that is, words not conforming to guidelines and patterns that have been taught. The first version is designed for Key Stage 1 pupils and the second for Key Stage 2 pupils. However, version 1 may be more appropriate for some children in Key Stage 2. They can be used in conjunction with the 'Words to practise' copymasters (see above).

Spelling strategies to use when writing

These provide a reminder of techniques, strategies and guidelines to use when attempting to spell words in writing. Again, version 1 is designed for Key Stage 1 pupils and version 2 for Key Stage 2 pupils. However, version 1 may be more appropriate for some children in Key Stage 2.

Responding to marking prompts

These establish a routine for pupils to correct spelling errors identified during marking. You can adapt the copymasters to fit with your school's marking policy.

Spelling certificates

These are provided to reward progress and encourage children to take pride in their spelling achievements.

Spelling 1: Additional word lists for pages 4 to 8

Name:				
Class:			Date:	

Spelling 1 page 4	Spelling 1 page 5	Spelling 1 page 6	Spelling 1 page 7	Spelling 1 page 8
man	flat	chat	yell	packs
yes	drip	such	frill	gifts
kit	frog	torch	spell	tricks
not	plum	arch	chill	pills
put	glad	chart	cliff	twins
van	melt	bench	stiff	kings
get	pond	shed	stuff	rocks
big	wind	shop	click	twigs
lot	lost	smash	chuck	nests
but	next	brush	shock	belts
rug	lump	crash	crack	prams
hop	chin	crush	clock	grunts
fox	print	cloth	dress	things
had	grand	bath	press	lumps
wet	frost	path	chess	shops

From: *Spelling: Teacher's Resource Book* by Carol Matchett (ISBN 978 07217 1219 2). Copyright © Schofield & Sims Ltd, 2013. Published by Schofield & Sims Ltd, Dogley Mill, Fenay Bridge, Huddersfield HD8 0NQ, UK (www.schofieldandsims.co.uk). This page may be photocopied after purchase for use within your school or institution only.

Spelling 1: Additional word lists for pages 10 to 17

Name:				
Class:			Date:	

Spelling 1 pages 10 and 14	Spelling 1 pages 11 and 14	Spelling 1 page 13	Spelling 1 page 16	Spelling 1 page 17
lifting	trainer	tray	fry	free
blocking	painter	spray	spy	meat
twisting	boiler	today	by	leaf
standing	joiner	brain	sty	peach
shocking	pointer	plain	spike	steam
costing	corner	hail	wine	stream
camping	starter	flake	pile	bleep
melting	marker	snake	alive	keep
passing	flicker	blame	ride	peep
bending	picker	date	bride	feel
clinging	litter	grave	slime	need
hunting	rocker	late	ripe	feed
smashing	tanker	hate	pipe	seed
spending	planter	gate	flight	week
grunting	conker	plate	slight	peek

From: **Spelling: Teacher's Resource Book** by Carol Matchett (ISBN 978 07217 1219 2). Copyright © Schofield & Sims Ltd, 2013. Published by Schofield & Sims Ltd, Dogley Mill, Fenay Bridge, Huddersfield HD8 0NQ, UK (www.schofieldandsims.co.uk). This page may be photocopied after purchase for use within your school or institution only.

Spelling 1: Additional word lists for pages 18 to 26

Name:	
Class:	Date:

Spelling 1 page 18	Spelling 1 page 20	Spelling 1 page 23	Spelling 1 page 25	Spelling 1 page 26
glow	toolbox	hound	batch	steams
crow	classroom	mound	thatch	reads
choke	toothbrush	around	clutch	saves
stroke	daylight	sprouts	crutch	starts
mole	starlight	clout	ditch	thanks
bone	pancake	stout	hitch	spends
stone	sunshade	snout	switch	rushes
dome	sunlight	mount	twitch	fishes
robe	starfish	foul	ouch	smashes
doze	lipstick	tower	pouch	passes
froze	postman	drown	inch	reaches
moat	popcorn	gown	clench	buzzes
gloat	windmill	crowd	punch	misses
oats	boatshed	owl	peach	marches
coast	boatman	powder	scrunch	pinches

From: **Spelling: Teacher's Resource Book** by Carol Matchett (ISBN 978 07217 1219 2). Copyright © Schofield & Sims Ltd, 2013. Published by Schofield & Sims Ltd, Dogley Mill, Fenay Bridge, Huddersfield HD8 0NQ, UK (www.schofieldandsims.co.uk). This page may be photocopied after purchase for use within your school or institution only.

Spelling 1: Additional word lists for pages 30 to 38

Name:				
Class:				Date:

Spelling 1 page 30	Spelling 1 page 32	Spelling 1 page 35	Spelling 1 page 36	Spelling 1 page 38
whack	hunted	rare	tusk	jolly
wheat	buzzed	glare	dusk	lorry
whine	dusted	blare	chunk	sorry
whip	landed	spare	stink	teddy
whimper	dashed	flare	plank	teeny
whizz	glowed	hare	blank	carry
whirl	harmed	aware	honk	Harry
whiff	reached	mare	kept	hurry
whopper	cracked	bare	kidnap	mummy
wink	limped	hairbrush	sketch	daddy
wake	kissed	upstairs	skim	thirty
west	winked	nowhere	scan	hockey
wipe			scatter	jockey
				money
				key

From: **Spelling: Teacher's Resource Book** by Carol Matchett (ISBN 978 07217 1219 2). Copyright © Schofield & Sims Ltd, 2013. Published by Schofield & Sims Ltd, Dogley Mill, Fenay Bridge, Huddersfield HD8 0NQ, UK (www.schofieldandsims.co.uk). This page may be photocopied after purchase for use within your school or institution only.

Spelling 2: Additional word lists for pages 4 to 10

Name:				
Class:			Date:	

Spelling 2 page 4	Spelling 2 page 5	Spelling 2 page 6	Spelling 2 page 7	Spelling 2 page 10
lane	crime	mow	street	snowing
cane	chime	mower	greet	peeling
drain	grime	below	sleet	calling
state	wise	rower	sleek	cheering
grate	prize	code	meek	wearing
scales	pride	rode	beef	turning
laid	spite	close	seem	joining
raid	spine	stone	lean	hiking
afraid	wipe	robe	mean	timing
daze	swipe	loan	bead	closing
amaze	thigh	foaming	lead	poking
shape	life	coal	reader	baking
grape	alive	gloat	clean	ruling
chase	spire	cloak	pleat	saving
case	wire	stoat	cheap	using
safe	bite	shoal		parking

From: **Spelling: Teacher's Resource Book** by Carol Matchett (ISBN 978 07217 1219 2). Copyright © Schofield & Sims Ltd, 2013. Published by Schofield & Sims Ltd, Dogley Mill, Fenay Bridge, Huddersfield HD8 0NQ, UK (www.schofieldandsims.co.uk). This page may be photocopied after purchase for use within your school or institution only.

Spelling 2: Additional word lists for pages 11 to 22

Name:

Class: Date:

Spelling 2 page 11	Spelling 2 page 12	Spelling 2 page 16	Spelling 2 page 17	Spelling 2 page 22
licked	nodding	clouds	sprays	stormy
pointed	yapping	brothers	keys	showy
marked	digging	shoes	plays	windy
sorted	hitting	slides	Sundays	soapy
soaked	getting	pies	tries	sporty
waited	tugging	cubes	spies	cheery
cooked	wagging	cones	flies	brainy
peeped	skipping	sizes	cries	scary
named	tipped	ashes	stories	rosy
smoked	patted	flashes	daisies	grimy
saved	rubbed	dresses	fairies	shady
voted	gripped	beaches	teddies	sloppy
timed	slapped	stitches	dollies	jammy
ruled	begged	scratches	chimneys	yappy
cared	prodded	brushes		

Spelling 2: Additional word lists for pages 23 to 34

Name:				
Class:			Date:	

Spelling 2 page 23	Spelling 2 page 24	Spelling 2 page 25	Spelling 2 page 28	Spelling 2 page 34
steeper	boastful	one	unpack	secret
greener	handful	won	unpick	puppet
slower	spoonful	to	unwind	kitten
clearer	mouthful	two	unroll	selfish
finer	shameful	for	unlike	fifteen
wiser	powerful	four	unfit	elbow
slimmer	charmless	I	uneven	dragon
fitter	endless	eye	unlit	lion
nearest	painless	son	unpaid	tower
proudest	harmless	sun	unclear	sofa
cheapest	thankless	road	unhelpful	invent
fairest	shameless	rode	unwise	bonfire
finest	powerless	beach		shower
wisest		beech		trumpet
reddest				

Spelling 3: Additional word lists for pages 4 to 10

Name:				
Class:				Date:

Spelling 3 page 4	Spelling 3 page 5	Spelling 3 page 6	Spelling 3 page 7	Spelling 3 page 10
pickle	huddle	borrow	final	snapped
thimble	settle	parrot	royal	chopped
dawdle	bobble	common	medal	trotted
jumble	skittle	dinner	dismal	robbed
humble	scuttle	sorrow	legal	dragged
fumble	nibble	narrow	hospital	tapped
trample	niggle	barrow	level	taped
tangle	raffle	glimmer	travel	dined
dimple	addle	bitter	hotel	scraped
pimple	guzzle	pepper	panel	stroked
jangle	fable	batter	rebel	tuned
bangle	cable	holly	gravel	juggled
couple	stable	ferry	easel	fizzled
	cradle	banner	tonsil	stumbled
			chapel	

Spelling 3: Additional word lists for pages 12 to 18

Name:	
Class:	Date:

Spelling 3 page 12	Spelling 3 page 13	Spelling 3 page 16	Spelling 3 page 17	Spelling 3 page 18
find – found	betrays	medic	expanse	outlaw
wind – wound	delays	frantic	expose	flaw
can – could	discovers	toxic	extent	raw
take – took	scurries	tropic	exclude	lawn
shake – shook	tidies	traffic	exotic	northern
rise – rose	marries	locket	taxis	haunted
slide – slid	doubles	socket	axe	scorching
shoot – shot	huddles	plucky	axle	bore
feed – fed	clutches	kipper	waxwork	seashore
spend – spent	stretches	kidney	hoax	dwarf
bend – bent	squashes	kindle	pixel	warp
sell – sold	preaches	kestrel	vixen	warship
weep – wept	perches	kebab	galaxy	board
sweep – swept	gushes	skipper	deluxe	roar
hear – heard	splashes	skunk		

From: **Spelling: Teacher's Resource Book** by Carol Matchett (ISBN 978 07217 1219 2). Copyright © Schofield & Sims Ltd, 2013. Published by Schofield & Sims Ltd, Dogley Mill, Fenay Bridge, Huddersfield HD8 0NQ, UK (www.schofieldandsims.co.uk). This page may be photocopied after purchase for use within your school or institution only.

Spelling 3: Additional word lists for pages 22 to 31

Name:				
Class:			Date:	

Spelling 3 page 22	Spelling 3 page 23	Spelling 3 page 24	Spelling 3 page 25	Spelling 3 page 31
chilly	glummer	firmly	wishful	Cinderella
grumpy	nosier	sternly	scornful	concert
thorny	sillier	warmly	wonderful	celebrate
fruity	fluffier	smoothly	thankless	grocer
jerky	heavier	smartly	tasteless	centigrade
greasy	nastier	swiftly	timeless	centipede
hazy	slimier	sadly	powerless	stencil
crazy	wettest	awkwardly	flawless	surface
juicy	maddest	lovely	braveness	gentleman
nervy	cuddliest	lately	lateness	digested
snappy	grumpiest	closely	kindness	tragic
furry	dirtiest	finely	placement	stranger
spotty	angriest	rudely	statement	germ
chatty	cosiest	gravely	payment	suggest
crumbly	squarest		pavement	cellar

From: **Spelling: Teacher's Resource Book** by Carol Matchett (ISBN 978 07217 1219 2). Copyright © Schofield & Sims Ltd, 2013. Published by Schofield & Sims Ltd, Dogley Mill, Fenay Bridge, Huddersfield HD8 0NQ, UK (www.schofieldandsims.co.uk). This page may be photocopied after purchase for use within your school or institution only.

Spelling 3: Additional word lists for pages 32 to 36

Name:		
Class:		Date:

Spelling 3 page 32	Spelling 3 page 34	Spelling 3 page 36
waist	repay	gesture
waste	reread	posture
deer	replay	culture
dear	refill	departure
peek	prejudge	torture
peak	prepay	pasture
rode	depart	venture
rowed	defuse	vulture
in	debug	pressure
inn	misspell	exposure
sight	misjudge	disclosure
site	mishap	displeasure
sore	misshape	injure
soar	disclose	figure
know		failure
no		

From: **Spelling: Teacher's Resource Book** by Carol Matchett (ISBN 978 07217 1219 2). Copyright © Schofield & Sims Ltd, 2013. Published by Schofield & Sims Ltd, Dogley Mill, Fenay Bridge, Huddersfield HD8 0NQ, UK (www.schofieldandsims.co.uk). This page may be photocopied after purchase for use within your school or institution only.

Spelling 4: Additional word lists for pages 4 to 13

Name:				
Class:				Date:

Spelling 4 page 4	Spelling 4 page 7	Spelling 4 page 10	Spelling 4 page 11	Spelling 4 pages 12 and 13
ball – bawl	chrysalis	circuses	pianos	vagueness
seen – scene	dynamic	choruses	banjos	vogue
you – ewe	dynamite	sandwiches	studios	morgue
rain – rein	megabyte	sheaves	patios	meringue
might – mite	gyrate	themselves	bongos	baguette
seem – seam	hyper	ourselves	cuckoos	guarantee
meter – metre	hyena	reefs	igloos	uniquely
tire – tyre	hyphen	proofs	tattoos	critique
roll – role	mystical	handcuffs	dominoes	mystique
wait – weight	stylish	briefs	torpedoes	boutique
steak – stake	symptom	mysteries	haloes	sequel
mare – mayor	synagogue	families	mangos/ mangoes	sequin
stile – style	syringe	injuries	cargos/cargoes	bouquet
rain – reign	tyre	pastries		racquet
	hymn	trophies		

From: **Spelling: Teacher's Resource Book** by Carol Matchett (ISBN 978 07217 1219 2). Copyright © Schofield & Sims Ltd, 2013. Published by Schofield & Sims Ltd, Dogley Mill, Fenay Bridge, Huddersfield HD8 0NQ, UK (www.schofieldandsims.co.uk). This page may be photocopied after purchase for use within your school or institution only.

Spelling 4: Additional word lists for pages 16 to 23

Name:				
Class:			Date:	

Spelling 4 page 16	Spelling 4 page 19	Spelling 4 page 20	Spelling 4 page 22	Spelling 4 page 23
bleary	subway	gravely	varied	central
spearmint	subdivide	sparkly	supplied	comical
shearing	submarine	strangely	damaged	critical
teary	substandard	entirely	exploded	magical
fearsome	subtitle	helpfully	measuring	removal
endearing	surname	gracefully	recycling	tropical
wearisome	misfortune	thankfully	approving	angelic
earnest	mismanaged	fatally	breathing	organic
earned	disinfected	brutally	continuing	suggestive
earthworm	dissolve	entirely	admitted	productive
learnt	disqualify	nobly	excelling	passive
nuclear	antidote	tickly	preferred	distinctive
heartache	cooperate	bristly	answered	impressive
hearten	coincidence	squiggly	listened	recovered
bearings	disapprove		limited	

Spelling 4: Additional word lists for pages 25 to 37

Name:				
Class:				Date:

Spelling 4 page 25	Spelling 4 page 29	Spelling 4 page 31	Spelling 4 page 35	Spelling 4 page 37
willingness	vibration	bendable	untouchable	transaction
foolishness	direction	disagreeable	unpleasantness	microfilm
tidiness	affection	questionable	recoverable	supernatural
clumsiness	addiction	unbelievable	disconnected	supernova
messiness	promotion	employable	displeasing	interchange
management	devotion	portable	pilgrimage	unique
replacement	completion	noticeable	disorderly	unify
employment	navigation	fashionable	repositioned	intercity
harpist	emotion	probable	uncertainty	biceps
motorist	election	understandable	suddenness	bifocal
violinist	repulsion	flexible	decomposing	binoculars
knighthood	occasion	legible	unattractive	triangle
earldom	mission		discontinued	tricycle
friendship	aggression		personalise	triple
shortage	profession			triplets

From: **Spelling: Teacher's Resource Book** by Carol Matchett (ISBN 978 07217 1219 2). Copyright © Schofield & Sims Ltd, 2013. Published by Schofield & Sims Ltd, Dogley Mill, Fenay Bridge, Huddersfield HD8 0NQ, UK (www.schofieldandsims.co.uk). This page may be photocopied after purchase for use within your school or institution only.

Spelling 5: Additional word lists for pages 6 to 13

Name:				
Class:			Date:	

Spelling 5 page 6	Spelling 5 page 7	Spelling 5 page 8	Spelling 5 page 11	Spelling 5 page 13
dollar	cutlery	contribution	flourish	tier
altar	crockery	revolution	clamour	review
pillar	grocery	competition	courtroom	siege
vinegar	embroidery	composition	nourishment	relieve
nectar	pottery	exhibition	gourmet	besiege
razor	slavery	separation	dour	retrieve
dictator	documentary	communication	sourness	cashier
investigator	infirmary	hesitation	savoury	experience
processor	centenary	toleration	endeavour	heir
navigator	anniversary	application	tambourine	reindeer
acre	territory	erosion	courgette	anxiety
massacre	lavatory	exclusion	adjourn	deceitful
sabre	inventory	comprehension	rigour	receiver
sombre	dormitory	depression	saviour	conceive
		percussion		conceited

Spelling 5: Additional word lists for pages 16 to 25

Name:				
Class:			Date:	

Spelling 5 page 16	Spelling 5 page 17	Spelling 5 page 18	Spelling 5 page 22	Spelling 5 page 25
civil	especially	gender	inattentive	horse
celery	atrocious	generate	inconsiderate	hoarse
cistern	vivacious	germinate	inefficient	rough
ceremony	ferocious	generation	inadequate	ruff
citrus	commercial	budget	inarticulate	bridal
cease	beneficial	gypsy	indecent	bridle
policy	conscience	geometry	immeasurable	shoot
cygnet	efficiency	vegetable	immaterial	chute
deceased	cucumber	college	impervious	air
urgency	cupid	gauge	irreplaceable	heir
cellophane	articulate	prestige	irremovable	tear
scarce	vaccine	ingenious	illegitimate	tier
discipline	acceptable			Sunday
specimen	access			sundae

From: **Spelling: Teacher's Resource Book** by Carol Matchett (ISBN 978 07217 1219 2). Copyright © Schofield & Sims Ltd, 2013. Published by Schofield & Sims Ltd, Dogley Mill, Fenay Bridge, Huddersfield HD8 0NQ, UK (www.schofieldandsims.co.uk). This page may be photocopied after purchase for use within your school or institution only.

Spelling 5: Additional word lists for pages 28 to 36

Name:				
Class:			Date:	

Spelling 5 page 28	Spelling 5 page 30	Spelling 5 page 31	Spelling 5 page 32	Spelling 5 page 36
tire	budgeted	scrupulous	considerable	intercom
time	orbited	tempestuous	tolerable	intersection
agree	profited	porous	recognisable	auditory
judge	profitable	monstrous	advisable	circumstances
inquire	galloped	glamorous	identifiable	circumstantial
retire	abandoned	rigorous	excusable	autopsy
contribute	developed	carnivorous	invincible	automation
assume	pocketed	advantageous	susceptible	aerodynamic
retrieve	omitted	grievous	destructible	pictograph
bereave	gossiped	boisterous	forcible	centurion
announce	uncommitted	dubious	capable	centenary
advance	regretted	anonymous	sociable	aquaplane
exercise	mimicked	ludicrous	peaceable	aeronaut
untie		ominous	serviceable	primate
		treacherous	chargeable	
		hilarious		

From: **Spelling: Teacher's Resource Book** by Carol Matchett (ISBN 978 07217 1219 2). Copyright © Schofield & Sims Ltd, 2013. Published by Schofield & Sims Ltd, Dogley Mill,
Fenay Bridge, Huddersfield HD8 0NQ, UK (www.schofieldandsims.co.uk). This page may be photocopied after purchase for use within your school or institution only.

Spelling 6: Additional word lists for pages 5 to 13

Name:				
Class:			Date:	

Spelling 6 page 5	Spelling 6 page 6	Spelling 6 page 10	Spelling 6 page 12	Spelling 6 page 13
unblemished	absolutely	comparative	acquaintance	eliminate
correspondence	extremely	competent	performance	privilege
disqualification	desperately	bachelor	attendance	aggravate
uninterrupted	separately	specimen	independence	appropriate
dishonourable	immediately	veterinary	convenience	occasional
restoration	agreeably	preliminary	inference	apparent
creativity	reliably	independence	existence	dissect
resignation	arguably	negotiate	emergency	college
acknowledgement	athletically	locomotive	efficiency	tobacco
advantageous	enthusiastically	apparently	consistency	millennium
unsuccessfully	energetically	amateur	frequency	accessory
unhurriedly	majestically	margarine	redundancy	accidentally
	essentially		vacancy	benefit
	occasionally		truancy	sheriff
	doubtfully		consultancy	

From: **Spelling: Teacher's Resource Book** by Carol Matchett (ISBN 978 07217 1219 2). Copyright © Schofield & Sims Ltd, 2013. Published by Schofield & Sims Ltd, Dogley Mill, Fenay Bridge, Huddersfield HD8 0NQ, UK (www.schofieldandsims.co.uk). This page may be photocopied after purchase for use within your school or institution only.

Spelling 6: Additional word lists for pages 16 to 25

Name:

Class: Date:

Spelling 6 page 16	Spelling 6 page 18	Spelling 6 page 20	Spelling 6 page 22	Spelling 6 page 25
ascend	re-enter	council	pedalling	maintain
asymmetrical	re-enact	counsel	unravelling	maintenance
elect	re-emerge	councillor	towelling	feasible
embalm	non-event	counsellor	channelling	feasibility
embark	co-ordinator	complement	spiralling	argue
embrace	co-starring	compliment	cancelling	argument
obstruct	ex-president	program	modelling	proceed
abstain	ex-manager	programme	appalling	procedure
absorb	ex-directory	lesson	yodelling	monstrous
corrupt	anti-wrinkle	lessen	snivelling	monstrosity
acquaint	anti-aircraft	idle	fulfilling	stable
dissatisfaction	de-icer	idol	panellist	stability
concise		forth	specialise	probable
socialise		fourth	finalise	probability
		dual	generalise	disable
		duel	fulfilment	disability

Schofield & Sims Spelling

Spelling 6: Additional word lists for pages 29 to 36

Name:

Class: Date:

Spelling 6 page 29	Spelling 6 page 30	Spelling 6 page 31	Spelling 6 page 32	Spelling 6 page 36
credentials	criminology	pheasant	sodium	Cyprus – Cypriot
discredited	microbiology	pharmacist	crematorium	Austria – Austrian
incredulous	terminology	phoney	planetarium	Switzerland – Swiss
spectre	program	epitaph	trillion	Belgium – Belgian
spectrum	barometer	chasm	union	Hungary – Hungarian
suspect	pedometer	chronic	battalion	Israel – Israeli
definition	astrodome	cholesterol	accordion	Ghana – Ghanaian
definitive	astronomic	rheumatism	legion	Trinidad – Trinidadian
finite	thermal	psychology	status	Barbados – Barbadian
traction	thermos	hydrogen	versus	Iraq – Iraqi
abstract	heptathlon	physician	thesaurus	Libya – Libyan
distraction	decathlon		prospectus	
edict	suicide			
verdict	insecticide			
dictator				

From: **Spelling: Teacher's Resource Book** by Carol Matchett (ISBN 978 07217 1219 2). Copyright © Schofield & Sims Ltd, 2013. Published by Schofield & Sims Ltd, Dogley Mill, Fenay Bridge, Huddersfield HD8 0NQ, UK (www.schofieldandsims.co.uk). This page may be photocopied after purchase for use within your school or institution only.

Spelling log 1: Mini spelling log

✂ -

Add a tick to the box on the right each time you use the word in your writing.

Add a tick to the box on the right each time you use the word in your writing.

My five 'need to know' words are:

My five 'need to know' words are:

← Fo

My five 'need to know' words are:

My mini spelling log

Name: _____

Class: _____ Date: _____

Add a tick to the box on the right each time you use the word in your writing.

↑
Fold

From: **Spelling: Teacher's Resource Book** by Carol Matchett (ISBN 978 07217 1219 2). Copyright © Schofield & Sims Ltd, 2013. Published by Schofield & Sims Ltd, Dogley Mill, Fenay Bridge, Huddersfield HD8 0NQ, UK (www.schofieldandsims.co.uk). This page may be photocopied after purchase for use within your school or institution only.

Spelling log 2: List format

Name:

Class:	Date:

These are the words I want to learn to spell:

Add a tick to the box on the right each time you use the word in your writing.

These are the words I want to learn to spell:

Add a tick to the box on the right each time you use the word in your writing.

Word sort 1

Name:	
Class:	Date:

Sort the words into two groups, so all the words in a group have the same spelling pattern or rule.

Write the rule or pattern at the top of each column. Then write the words in the correct box.

Odd ones that do not follow the rule:

Word sort 2

Name:	
Class:	Date:

Sort the words into three groups, so all the words in a group have the same spelling pattern or rule.

Write the rule or pattern at the top of each column. Then write the words in the correct box.

Odd ones that do not follow the rule:

Word sort 3

Name:	
Class:	Date:

Sort the words into four groups, so all the words in a group have the same spelling pattern or rule.

Write the rule or pattern at the top of each box. Then write the words in the correct box.

Word collector 1

Name:	
Class:	Date:

See how many words you can find with the spelling pattern _____.

Write the words on the scroll.

My collection of _____ words

Word collector 2

Name:	
Class:	Date:

Build a wall of words with the spelling pattern _____.

See how many words you can find for your word wall.

Write each word on a brick in the wall.

Colour the brick when you can spell the word.

From: *Spelling: Teacher's Resource Book* by Carol Matchett (ISBN 978 07217 1219 2). Copyright © Schofield & Sims Ltd, 2013. Published by Schofield & Sims Ltd, Dogley Mill, Fenay Bridge, Huddersfield HD8 0NQ, UK (www.schofieldandsims.co.uk). This page may be photocopied after purchase for use within your school or institution only.

Words to practise: Spelling practice ladders

Name:
Class:	Date:

Write the word you want to practise at the top of the ladder.

Practise saying and writing it five times. Then cover the word and see if you can spell it.

From: *Spelling: Teacher's Resource Book* by Carol Matchett (ISBN 978 07217 1219 2). Copyright © Schofield & Sims Ltd, 2013. Published by Schofield & Sims Ltd, Dogley Mill, Fenay Bridge, Huddersfield HD8 0NQ, UK (www.schofieldandsims.co.uk). This page may be photocopied after purchase for use within your school or institution only.

Target reminder 1: Fold-over version

I should remember this target every time I do a piece of writing.

Some examples to help me remember:

My target is to _____

Class:	Date:
Name:	

Fold →

Name:	
Class:	Date:

My target is to _____

Some examples to help me remember:

I should remember this target every time I do a piece of writing.

From: **Spelling: Teacher's Resource Book** by Carol Matchett (ISBN 978 07217 1219 2). Copyright © Schofield & Sims Ltd, 2013. Published by Schofield & Sims Ltd, Dogley Mill, Fenay Bridge, Huddersfield HD8 0NQ, UK (www.schofieldandsims.co.uk). This page may be photocopied after purchase for use within your school or institution only.

Target reminder 2: Placemat version

Name:

Class:

Date:

My target is to _____

Here are some examples to help me remember my target:

I should remember this target every time I do a piece of writing.

Target reminder 3: Fold-over mini-target version

Tick a box each time you spell a word correctly in your writing.

_____

_____

_____

_____

These are your target words. Remember to spell them correctly when you are writing.

Class:	Date:
Name:	

Fold →

Name:	
Class:	Date:

These are your target words. Remember to spell them correctly when you are writing.

_____

_____

_____

_____

Tick a box each time you spell a word correctly in your writing.

Words to practise: My tricky words

Name:	
Class:	Date:

Look through your writing for words that you keep spelling wrongly.
Find the correct spelling of these words and copy them into the first column.

Learn to spell these words. Take the word apart and find the tricky bit.
Remember, cover and write it.

Read and look.	Write it. Take the word apart.	Write it. Find the tricky bit.	Remember it. Cover it. Write it.	Check. ✓

Make up your own spelling sentences to help you practise your tricky words.

_____

_____

_____

_____

From: **Spelling: Teacher's Resource Book** by Carol Matchett (ISBN 978 07217 1219 2). Copyright © Schofield & Sims Ltd, 2013. Published by Schofield & Sims Ltd, Dogley Mill,
Fenay Bridge, Huddersfield HD8 0NQ, UK (www.schofieldandsims.co.uk).

Words to practise: My topic words

Name:				
Class:			Date:	

Collect examples of words that you need to write in another subject.
Copy the correct spelling of these words into the first column.

Learn to spell the words. Take the word apart and find any tricky bits.
Remember, cover and write it.

Read and look.	Write it. Take the word apart.	Write it. Find the tricky bit.	Remember it. Cover it. Write it.	Check. ✓

Make up your own spelling sentences to help you practise these topic words.

_____

_____

_____

_____

From: **Spelling: Teacher's Resource Book** by Carol Matchett (ISBN 978 07217 1219 2). Copyright © Schofield & Sims Ltd, 2013. Published by Schofield & Sims Ltd, Dogley Mill, Fenay Bridge, Huddersfield HD8 0NQ, UK (www.schofieldandsims.co.uk). This page may be photocopied after purchase for use within your school or institution only.

Learning and practising tricky words 1

1. **Look** at the word and **read** it.

2. **Copy** the word carefully.

3. **Take the word apart**. Say the sounds and point to the letters.

4. **Find the tricky part**. That's the bit that catches you out.
   Write over it in colour.

5. **Choose a memory trick** to help remember the correct spelling.

6. Use your memory trick to help you **write** the word three to five times.
   Check that you spell it correctly each time.

7. Now **cov**er the word, **write** it and **check** it.

8. Keep **practising** to make sure it sticks.

Memory tricks

- **Say it as it's spelt**, for example: say **w-a-s** not 'w-o-s'.

- **Say the syllables**, for example: say Wed/**nes**/day.

- **Chant the letter names**, for example: **o-u-t spells out**.

- **Spell it like ...** think of another word with the same spelling pattern, for example: **they** is like **the**.

- **Find a word within a word**, for example: **eat** is in gr**eat**.

Learning and practising tricky words 2

1. **Look** at the word, **read** it and **copy** it carefully.

2. **Take it apart**. For a short word, say the separate sounds. For a longer word, take it apart syllable by syllable or find the base word and affixes attached to it.

3. Now **find the tricky part** – that's the part with the unexpected spelling that catches you out. **Write** over it in colour.

4. **Choose a memory strategy** to help remember the correct spelling, especially the tricky bit. (You will find some suggestions in the box below.)

5. Use the memory strategy to **write** the word five times. **Check** it each time.

6. Now, **cover** the word, **write** it and **check** it.

7. Keep **practising** to make sure it sticks.

Memory strategies to try

- **Say it as it's spelt**, for example: say **k-nock** rather than 'nock'.

- **Say the syllables**, for example: say **Wed/nes/day**.

- **Chant the letter names** as you write the word or the tricky part, for example: **o-u-g-h**.

- **Spell it like ... (analogy)**, make a link to another word with the same spelling pattern and practise writing the words together, for example: **could would**.

- Use a **memory trick** like find a 'word within a word' (for example, **pie** in **pieces**) or making up a mnemonic (for example, rhythm: **h**ow **y**ou **t**ap, **h**um, **m**ove).

Top tips

1. Keep looking at the word, then cover it and picture it in your head until you can 'see' the word and know when it looks correct.

2. Trace the word in the air or on paper. Write it lots and lots of times until you get a feel for the word and can write it without thinking.

From: **Spelling: Teacher's Resource Book** by Carol Matchett (ISBN 978 07217 1219 2). Copyright © Schofield & Sims Ltd, 2013. Published by Schofield & Sims Ltd, Dogley Mill, Fenay Bridge, Huddersfield HD8 0NQ, UK (www.schofieldandsims.co.uk). This page may be photocopied after purchase for use within your school or institution only.

Spelling strategies to use when writing 1

What can I do to help me spell a word?

If it's a long word, say the syllables and then spell each syllable.

Say the sounds. Write the letters that make each sound.

Think of a word you know that sounds the same.

Have a go. See if it looks correct.

Think about how word endings are spelt.

Try two spellings and see which one looks correct.

Look in your spelling book or on word lists and displays in the classroom.

*From: **Spelling: Teacher's Resource Book** by Carol Matchett (ISBN 978 07217 1219 2). Copyright © Schofield & Sims Ltd, 2013. Published by Schofield & Sims Ltd, Dogley Mill, Fenay Bridge, Huddersfield HD8 0NQ, UK (www.schofieldandsims.co.uk). This page may be photocopied after purchase for use within your school or institution only.*

Spelling strategies to use when writing 2

How can I spell a word that I am not sure of?

Say the sounds and think about the most likely way to spell the sounds.

Say each syllable clearly and spell each syllable in turn.

If there is more than one possible spelling, write them both and see which looks correct.

Think about other words that sound the same that you do know how to spell. Follow the pattern.

Break the word down into a root word and affixes. Then build it up to spell it.

Use the rules you know for adding suffixes.

Think about related words that give a clue to the spelling.

Think about endings. Remember they are not always spelt as they sound.

Check in your spelling book or on word lists.

Look for the word in a dictionary.

Responding to marking

When your teacher has marked your writing there might be some words underlined. This means that those words were spelt wrongly.

Follow these instructions for what you should do.

> ## Look for words that your teacher has marked as wrong.
>
> This means you should be able to spell the word correctly.

> ## Look at how you spelt the word and work out where the mistake is.
>
> If you are not sure, look in your spelling book. You might find the word there, or a pattern or rule that will help you.

> ## When you know the correct spelling, write it in.
>
> Write it either above the mistake or in the margin.

> ## Now make sure you don't make the same mistake again. Practise writing and saying the correct spelling five times.

From: *Spelling: Teacher's Resource Book* by Carol Matchett (ISBN 978 07217 1219 2). Copyright © Schofield & Sims Ltd, 2013. Published by Schofield & Sims Ltd, Dogley Mill, Fenay Bridge, Huddersfield HD8 0NQ, UK (www.schofieldandsims.co.uk). This page may be photocopied after purchase for use within your school or institution only.

Spelling certificates

Well done!

....

You are a super speller
and this certificate
is awarded to you for

....

Congratulations!
This certificate has been awarded to

....

for special achievement in spelling
and in particular for

....

Part two:
Assessment and record-keeping resources

1   Introduction to Part two

In this part of the book you will find resources to support the 'assess' stage and your ongoing, weekly and periodic assessment of spelling, undertaken as part of the **Spelling** programme. The resources cover:

- ongoing assessment (with target and progress tracking sheets)
- weekly assessment (with 'Dictation assessment sheets')
- periodic assessment (with cloze-style 'Dictation tests').

In addition, materials are provided for the analysis of spelling errors in independent writing.

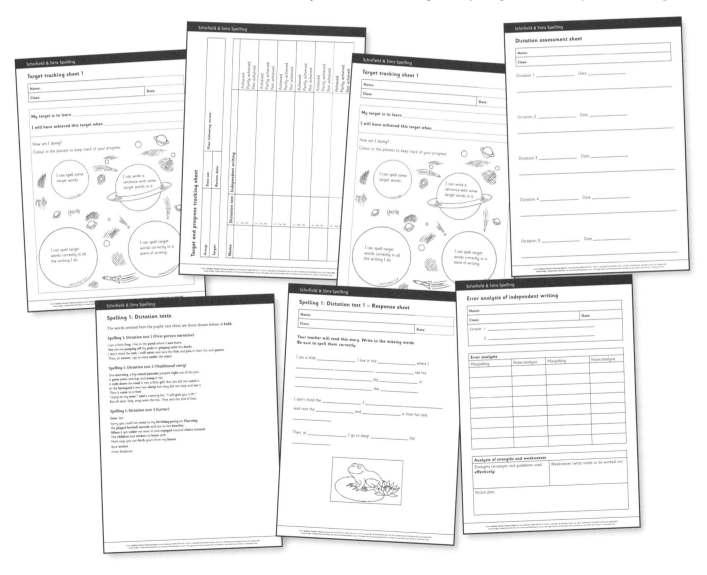

2 The assessment process

Ongoing assessment

Ongoing assessment should focus on how well pupils have grasped spelling rules, guidelines and patterns. It should cover both the strategies already introduced in the pupil books and those which are currently being worked on.

Main targets

To help focus your assessments you should set clear spelling targets and share these with the pupils. Although usually set as group targets, they may be used as whole-class targets if appropriate. All the targets should reflect the guidelines and patterns currently being taught and practised in the pupil book, but their focus should be wider than the weekly focus.

Some examples of typical targets might be:

● I will use the rules for adding **ed** and **ing** when I am writing. (Year 2)

● I will learn to spell words with unstressed vowels and unstressed endings and then spell them correctly in my writing. (Year 5)

Once set, the spelling targets should be applied to all writing carried out by the pupils over a period of three to six weeks. If you and the pupils are to monitor the application of the targets, it is essential that they are recorded. You should make a note of every spelling target on the 'Target and progress tracking sheet' and on the pupils' 'Target tracking sheet'. These sheets are then used to record evidence of progress towards the targets from the weekly dictation assessments and independent writing.

Full instructions for use of the 'Target and progress tracking sheet' copymaster, together with a completed example, can be found on pages 56–7.

Mini-targets

An additional target, referred to as a 'mini-target', may be set in the same half-term period. This might relate to words with a more specific pattern or to learning a set of specific tricky or topic words. A mini-target might be, 'I will spell these words correctly when I write a story', followed by a list of words.

Weekly assessment

The dictation sentences, which form the basis of the weekly spelling assessments, are found in the 'Teaching notes' section of the **Teacher's Guide**. These short dictations include target words relating to the current focus, underlined for your quick reference. In addition, they sometimes include words introduced previously, to check that learning has been retained.

A 'Dictation assessment sheet' copymaster is provided. Full instructions for use, together with guidelines for completion of the assessment, can be found on page 50.

Periodic assessment

Included in Part two are all the materials needed for administering longer dictated tests. Each test assesses 20 words and consists of a cloze-style passage, with target words to be written in by pupils as you read the passage aloud.

There are three cloze tests for each pupil book, designed as end-of-term assessments, one per term. The tests cover a range of words which are representative of the cumulative learning that should have taken place up to that point. Their purpose is:

● to check that spelling knowledge is being retained and transferred to long-term memory

● to give a more objective view of what each pupil knows in relation to expected progress.

Full instructions for carrying out the tests can be found on page 51.

Error analysis sheet

You will also find 'Error analysis sheets' for use with all the periodic tests. These can be used to help you identify individual or group weaknesses and find areas that need to be revisited. You can use this information to adjust your plans for future teaching: for example, you might decide to focus on a particular area during a class revision week.

Full instructions for carrying out an analysis can be found on page 52.

Analysing spelling in independent writing

An error analysis sheet for assessing spelling within samples of independent writing is also provided. This formal analysis of independent writing is only carried out occasionally and is not usually necessary for all pupils: this makes it quite distinct from ongoing assessment. The more formal approach can be useful, however, in helping you to identify particular problem areas for pupils who are struggling. Discussion with the pupil, during or after the writing process, about why he or she made a particular spelling choice can help to explain the cause of problems and assist you in setting individual targets.

The 'Error analysis of independent writing' record sheet can be found at the end of the book and full instructions for carrying out an analysis of independent writing are given on page 54.

3 Using the assessment resources

Ongoing assessment

Administering the weekly dictation assessment

- Find the dictation sentence in the 'Teaching notes' section of the **Teacher's Guide**.
- Hand out copies of the 'Dictation assessment sheet' copymaster. This has space for five dictation assessments so will form a record of a pupil's performance over several weeks. A new copy will be needed for each section of the pupil book.
- Read the dictation sentence aloud.
- Read the sentence again, breaking it into short meaningful chunks. Say each chunk several times, giving pupils time to write and check the words. You should say any punctuation marks – although punctuation is not part of the assessment, using it should be seen as a natural part of writing sentences and pupils should include it.
- Read the sentence through once more. Ask pupils to do a final check of their spelling, remembering what they have been learning in class.

Class marking of the weekly dictation assessment

- Once the dictation is completed, pupils can work in pairs to check each other's work.
- Write or display the sentence on the board. Ask the pupils to check the sentence word by word, putting a small tick above each correct word and underlining any errors.
- Discuss errors. Your discussions should help pupils to understand why the errors occurred: for example, because a particular rule or pattern has been forgotten.
- Give pupils time to practise any words spelt incorrectly. For example, you might ask them to find the correct spelling in their pupil books and then use a 'Words to practise: Spelling practice ladders' copymaster to write it a number of times.

Following up the weekly assessment

- Give pupils the opportunity to reflect on their learning and to decide whether or not they are ready to tick the 'I can …' statement/s at the foot of the pupil book page. It may be that they need more practice.
- Make notes on a photocopy of the group 'Target and progress tracking sheet'. Use a tick to show that all words are correct, a question mark if there is one error (make a note of the word spelt incorrectly) and a cross if more than one of the focus words is spelt incorrectly.
- Use this information to decide whether the whole group or selected individuals within the group need an additional session to revise or recap the focus. If many of the pupils have made errors, you will need to revise the guideline or spelling pattern before moving on.

Periodic assessment

Using the cloze dictation test

There are three tests for each of the pupil books; one test for each term. You do not need to use all three, but it is important to use the test appropriate for the term: for example, Dictation test 1 towards the end of term 1. This is to avoid pupils being tested on words with patterns or guidelines they have not yet been taught.

Administering the cloze dictation test

- Find the dictation passage for the relevant book and term. This gives the complete version of the passage, with the target words shown in **bold**.
- Locate the relevant 'Dictation response sheet' copymaster. This provides the same passage with blank spaces for the pupils to write in the given words. Make enough copies for the group or class.
- Decide whether to present the test informally, or to administer it under more formal test conditions in order to familiarise pupils with such situations.
- Hand out the 'Dictation response sheets'. Explain the purpose of the assessment, tell the pupils that they will be required to spell the missing words correctly, and remind them to think about what they have learnt as this will help them to spell the words.
- Tell the pupils that you are going to read the complete passage once through before the test begins. This will familiarise them with the subject matter and establish the context.
- Just before reading the passage again, explain to the pupils that the test will now begin. Tell them that if they make a mistake or change their mind about an answer they should cross it out clearly and write in the new spelling.
- Read the passage through for a second time, pausing at each word appearing in **bold**. Give the pupils time to write and then check the word. Make sure that the pupils write each word on a separate line, particularly if two words come together.
- Repeat the target words as many times as necessary but do not say them in a way that helps with spelling them.

Marking

You can either mark the test yourself using the teacher dictation text, or discuss and write the words on the board so that pupils can check each other's work. Award one mark for the correct spelling of a whole word.

Follow-up

The results of the cloze dictation test will help you identify individual or group weaknesses and areas that need to be revisited. You should adjust your planning and teaching to take account of this. For example, you might organise a revision week at the end of a section of the pupil book to revisit a particular focus that has not been retained.

Error analysis sheet

An 'Error analysis sheet' is provided for each test to help you identify significant problem areas for individuals or groups, so you can decide on areas that need to be revisited.

An example of a completed error analysis sheet is given opposite. As you can see, it lists the words tested and gives the 'assessment focus' for each word – that is, the pattern or guideline that is being tested. In many cases there is more than one focus for each word. For example, the word **suitable** is testing both the **ui** spelling of the long 'oo' sound and each pupil's knowledge of the **able** suffix.

Completing the error analysis sheet

- Enter pupils' names across the top of the sheet. There are spaces for six pupils; if the whole class has sat the same test then more copies of the sheet will be needed.

- Go through the marked test papers and enter X in the appropriate box if the pupil has spelt a word or part of a word incorrectly. It is important to look at where in the word an error occurs in order to complete the analysis sheet accurately. For example, if the word **generous** is spelt **genarous**, the error is in the unstressed middle syllable rather than the soft **g** or **ous** ending.

- When all the pupils' test results have been entered, the errors for each word or part of a word can be added up; this can be done across all the sheets if more than one has been used. These totals give you an overview of strengths and weaknesses across the group or class and reveal priority areas for revision and reinforcement.

In the completed example, some words are spelt correctly by all or most of the pupils. However, over half of the group have problems with the unstressed vowels in the words **generous** and **benefits**. A large number of errors indicates that the area needs to be revisited. In the example given, the teacher has identified unstressed vowels and syllables as an area that needs further attention.

Planning further teaching

It is important to adjust your teaching plans in the light of the information obtained from the cloze dictation test. You might do this by:

- looking to see whether the same focus occurs again in the relevant pupil book: a useful feature of **Schofield & Sims Spelling** is that repetition and revision are built in, in order to constantly reinforce and embed pupils' spelling knowledge

- organising a special revision session in which you go over the guideline or strategy once again

- using the general copymaster resources to put together your own tailor-made revision week that addresses the problem areas you have identified; you might do this instead of asking pupils to work through the revision page at the end of the pupil book section.

Spelling 4: Test 3 – Error analysis sheet

Teacher's name: Mr Watts

Class: 3   Date: 18/10

Word	Focus	Simon	Jess	Katie	Luke	Jae	Lisa	Total errors per focus
realise	root word **real**							
	suffix **ise**							
forgotten	adding **en**							
	double consonant							
bicycle	root **bi**							
	cycle							
valuable	root word **value**							
	suffix **able**	x uble		x				2
	drop **e**				x	x		2
possession	**ssion** spelling of 'shun'			x sion				1
	root word **possess**		x				x	2
obviously	**ious** ending	x		x				2
	suffix **ly**							
machine	**ch** spelling of 'sh'							
	ine							
suitable	**ui** spelling of 'oo'							
	suffix **able**							
different	syllables (**fer** unstressed)	x			x		x	3
	double **f**							
	ent ending							
redesigned	root word **sign**							
	adding affixes		x	x				2
generous	soft **g**							
	unstressed syllable (**er**)	x	x		x			3
	ous ending							
benefits	unstressed middle vowel	x		x		x	x	4
medical	**med-ic**							
	suffix **al**							
education	suffix **ation**							
transport	roots **trans/port**							
families	unstressed **i**		x		x		x	3
	plural (**y** to **ies**)	x						1
business	root word **busy**							
	suffix **ness**							
	y to 'i'							
international	**inter**	x						1
	nation							
	suffix **al**							
improving	**im/prove**							
	adding **ing** (drop **e**)							
interest	syllables (unstressed **er**)		x					1
Total errors per pupil								

Analysing errors in independent writing

You will only need to do an analysis of errors in independent writing occasionally and it is not usually necessary for all pupils. Its purpose is to identify problem areas for pupils who are struggling. It can help you decide on the pupil's strengths and weaknesses and decide what special action might be required.

A copymaster to help you carry out an error analysis of independent writing is provided and an example of a completed error analysis sheet is given opposite.

How to carry out an error analysis

- Select a sample or samples of the pupil's independent writing. Choose samples that fairly represent the pupil's spelling. Think carefully about the context and the amount of support the pupil had available when writing.

- Identify errors in those words that you would expect the pupil to know, rather than those that feature patterns the pupil has not yet been taught. Record the misspellings on a photocopy of the error analysis sheet.

- Make notes about where in the word the error occurs and any strategies that have been used, whether successfully or unsuccessfully. You might find it useful to talk to the pupil about how he or she went about spelling the word or why a particular spelling choice was made. This is best done at the time of writing or directly after and can often help to reveal the cause of problems.

- Look for any patterns revealed in the misspellings. Record both strengths (what the pupil knows and the strategies that he or she has used successfully) and weaknesses (the problems that are resulting in the most serious misspellings).

- Use the strengths and weaknesses to decide on priority areas and how and when to tackle them. For example, you can see in the completed example opposite that the teacher has decided to tackle the spelling of word endings through guided writing. The teacher is going to use the strategy of getting the pupil to 'say it as it's spelt'. This means that the pupil will be asked to stress the ending so that the correct spelling is clearly heard, rather than saying it as it would normally be pronounced.

- To help focus the pupil on the importance of using this strategy, it can be set as an individual target which applies to all the writing that he or she undertakes.

Error analysis of independent writing

Name: Jack	
Class: 3	Date: 10/11

Samples: 1. <u>Independent writing – story</u>

2. <u>Independent Recount – Bonfire Night</u>

Error analysis

Misspelling	Notes/analysis	Misspelling	Notes/analysis
verry	double r	massif	✓ mass x ive ending
persun	✓ vowel spelling x ending	cousons	✓ ou spelling x ending
spoocy	x c/k ✓ oo ✓ y -suffix	amasing	(amazing) s/z
ligth	visual error? letters in wrong order	enything	Tricky word
curtins	✓ correct word x ending	rockit	et ending
minits	Tricky words		
squaer	Letters in wrong order. Visual?		
exited	missing soft c ✓ ex ted		

Analysis of strengths and weaknesses

Strengths (strategies and guidelines used effectively)
- Phonically plausible
- Correct choice of many vowel sounds
- adding ed, ing

Weaknesses (what needs to be worked on)
- Tends to spell word endings as they sound
- Letter confusions eg s/z c/k
- Sometimes gets right letters in the wrong order eg ligth

Action plan
- Tackle word endings in guided writing. Use strategy of 'say it as it's spelt' e.g. say 'per/son'.
- Encourage Jack to look at his spellings to see if they look right (e.g. light, square)
- Set 'minutes' and 'anything' as tricky words to learn.

4

Using the record sheets

The 'Target and progress tracking sheet'

The purpose of the 'Target and progress tracking' sheet is to record the spelling targets set for a group and to summarise evidence of progress towards the targets. This evidence will come from the weekly assessments and from pupils' independent writing. An example of a completed sheet is shown opposite.

The 'Target and progress tracking sheet' is used like this.

- The spelling target set for the group is recorded at the top of the sheet, together with the date set and a date for review. In the completed example opposite, the target is set for a four-week period while the pupils are working on the relevant pages of **Spelling** 2.

- After each weekly dictation, note any evidence of progress towards the target. A tick indicates that all words are spelt correctly; a question mark denotes one error; a cross shows that more than one error has been made.

- The weekly dictation is not the only source of evidence of a pupil's progress towards the target. You should also look for evidence in the pupil's independent writing. Sometimes you will record examples of words spelt correctly that mark significant progress towards the target. At other times you will note misspellings, which indicate that a rule is not yet being applied to writing.

- Sometimes you may refer to a writing sample. This is a copy of a piece of independent writing with words highlighted to show progress towards the target. The highlighting is done with the co-operation of the pupil, so that he or she is aware of progress. If you prefer, pupils can track their own progress using their own 'Target tracking sheet'.

- At the end of the set period, record whether the target has been achieved, partly achieved or not achieved. In the example, the teacher has noted that he or she will keep reinforcing the target from time to time in shared and guided writing.

Pupils' 'Target tracking sheet'

Copymasters are provided for two versions of the pupils' 'Target tracking sheet', the first version for Key Stage 1 and the second for Key Stage 2. In the simpler version, the target is recorded and progress is tracked by colouring in planets as steps towards the target are achieved.

In the more complex version, the pupil is required to note down specific evidence to show that he or she is working towards the target: for example, reference might be made to a piece of writing in which the pupil has spelt focus words correctly.

Target and progress tracking sheet

Group: Orange	Date set: 01/11	Plan following review: Keep reinforcing in shared and guided
Target: Use rules for adding ed and ing	Review date: 25/11	writing, particularly doubling and y to i

Name	Dictation test	Independent writing	
Sarah	1. ✓ 2. ✓ 3. ? skipd 4. ? cride	10/11 ✓ called helped lived making x tierd 18/11 x grabed ✓ swimming 24/11 ✓ see highlighted sample	Achieved Partly achieved ✓ Not achieved
Mark	1. ✓ 2. ✓ 3. ✓ 4. ✓	10/11 ✓ shouting jumped pushed driving x snaped stoped 18/11 ✓ dropped grinned 24/11 see sample	Achieved ✓ Partly achieved Not achieved
Michael	1. ✓ 2. ✓ 3. ✓ 4. ✓	10/11 ✓ picked playing singing locked x opend 18/11 ✓ tripped 24/11 see sample	Achieved ✓ Partly achieved Not achieved
Alex	1. ✓ 2. ? shoutid 3. 4. ? dryed	10/11 x drest dartid stept ✓ pulled pushed cleaned 18/11 ✓ started 24/11 see sample	Achieved Partly achieved ✓ Not achieved
Natalie	1. ✓ 2. ✓ 3. waged 4. ?	10/11 ✓ played saved trying making stopped x stard cryd 18/11 floped x ✓ hopping 24/11 see sample	Achieved Partly achieved ✓ Not achieved
Becky	1. ✓ 2. ✓ 3. ✓ 4. ✓	10/11 ✓ shouting making jumped lived stayed x followd 18/11 stopped dropped 24/11 ✓ see highlighted sample	Achieved ✓ Partly achieved Not achieved

Target tracking sheet 1

Name:

Class: **Date:**

My target is to learn _____

I will have achieved this target when _____

How am I doing?

Colour in the planets to keep track of your progress.

I can spell some target words.

I can write a sentence with some target words in it.

I can spell target words correctly in all the writing I do.

I can spell target words correctly in a piece of writing.

Target tracking sheet 2

Name:

Class: **Date:**

My target is _____

I will have achieved this target when _____

Progress towards my target

Where's the evidence? Make a note of the evidence that shows you are moving towards your target. This might be a spelling test or a piece of writing.

Evidence 1

Evidence 2

Evidence 3

Evidence 4

Target reviewed (date) _____

I can _____

My comment:

Teacher comment:

Target and progress tracking sheet

Group:	Date set:		Plan following review:
Target:		Review date:	

Name	Dictation test	Independent writing			
	1. 2. 3.		Achieved	Partly achieved	Not achieved
	1. 2. 3.		Achieved	Partly achieved	Not achieved
	1. 2. 3.		Achieved	Partly achieved	Not achieved
	1. 2. 3.		Achieved	Partly achieved	Not achieved
	1. 2. 3.		Achieved	Partly achieved	Not achieved
	1. 2. 3.		Achieved	Partly achieved	Not achieved

Spelling 1: Dictation tests

The words omitted from the pupils' test sheet are those shown below in **bold**.

Spelling 1: Dictation test 1 (First-person narrative)

I am a little **frog**. I live in the **pond** where I **was born**.
You see me **jumping off** lily **pads** or **playing with** the **ducks**.
I don't mind the **rain**. I **still swim** and race the **fish** and **join** in their fun and **games**.
Then, at **sunset**, I go to sleep **under** the **stars**.

Spelling 1: Dictation test 2 (Traditional story)

One **morning**, a big **round pancake** jumped **right** out of the pan.
It **grew arms** and legs and **away** it ran.
A **mile down** the **road** it met a little **girl**. But she did not **catch** it.
In the **farmyard** it met two **sheep** but they did not stop and **eat** it.
Then it **came** to a **river**.
"Jump on my **nose**," **said** a cunning fox. "I will **give** you a lift."
But oh dear. Snip, snap went the fox. That was the end of that.

Spelling 1: Dictation test 3 (Letter)

Dear Joe

Sorry you could not **come** to my **birthday party** on **Thursday**.
We **played football outside** and ate on the **benches**.
When it got **colder** we went in and **enjoyed** musical **chairs instead**.
The **children** had **stickers** to **leave** with.
Mum says you can **fetch** yours from my **house**.

Best **wishes**

From Shabnam

From: **Spelling: Teacher's Resource Book** by Carol Matchett (ISBN 978 07217 1219 2). Copyright © Schofield & Sims Ltd, 2013. Published by Schofield & Sims Ltd, Dogley Mill, Fenay Bridge, Huddersfield HD8 0NQ, UK (www.schofieldandsims.co.uk). This page may be photocopied after purchase for use within your school or institution only.

Spelling 2: Dictation tests

The words omitted from the pupils' test sheet are those shown below in **bold**.

Spelling 2: Dictation test 1 (Description of visit to fairground)

"Are you **ready** to go to the **fairground**?" **asked** Dad.

Yes! We all **clapped** our hands and **cheered**.

What a time we had! **Shooting along** on the big dipper, **sliding** down the helter-skelter, **waving** from the big **wheel**. It was **great**.

We **tried** to **dodge** Dad on the **bumper** cars but it was no **use**. He was too good.

There was just time to each have a **turn** at **knocking** coconuts from the **shy before** it was time to go.

Spelling 2: Dictation test 2 (Extract from story)

Charlie the **cheeky monkey** hid in the **branches** of the tree.
He **dropped** a coconut on the lion as he **walked** by.
"Whoops, **careless** of me," said Charlie.
He **squirted water** at the leopard and her **babies** sleeping **nearby**.
"**Watch** out," said Charlie in a **helpful** sort of **voice**.
He **squashed** up his **ripest** banana to **throw** at the **giraffe**.
But **meanwhile**, Charlie's mum came up **behind** Charlie.
"Charlie, you **should** not do that," she said.

Spelling 2: Dictation test 3 (Pupil's letter giving account of a Victorian school)

17th October 1894

Dear Harry

I thought you would like to hear about the **village school**. That is where I learn the **alphabet** and I do this **fancy handwriting**. I keep a rag in my **pocket** so I can clean my **slate**. The thing I like best is listening to **stories**.

There is a **stove** in the **middle** of the room so that is the **warmest** place to sit in the **winter**. The **windows** are high up so we **can't** see out.

Did I **mention** the **teacher**? She is **scary**. Once my **page** of sums **displeased** her and she gave me a **caning**.

*From: **Spelling: Teacher's Resource Book** by Carol Matchett (ISBN 978 07217 1219 2). Copyright © Schofield & Sims Ltd, 2013. Published by Schofield & Sims Ltd, Dogley Mill, Fenay Bridge, Huddersfield HD8 0NQ, UK (www.schofieldandsims.co.uk). This page may be photocopied after purchase for use within your school or institution only.*

Spelling 3: Dictation tests

The words omitted from the pupils' test sheet are those shown below in **bold**.

Spelling 3: Dictation test 1 (Story extract)

The boy **climbed** over the wall and **scrambled** down into the **hidden** garden. Here the trees were as tall as **eight** men. **Poppies** with **petals** like velvet swayed in the breeze.

Raindrops **tumbled** from the trees like a **fountain**, **sparkling** in the now **brilliant August** sunshine.

Rabbits **scurried** away as the boy **stepped** on the **stony** path. The **chorus** of birdsong **faded**.

Even the insects **wriggled** away and hid under **daisies**, **staring** at this **stranger**.

Spelling 3: Dictation test 2 (Traditional story)

Who was hiding in the cave?

"Stay away or I will **trample** you to dust," warned a **fearful** voice from inside the cave.

When they **heard** that, all the other **animals trembled**.

The mice began the **panic**. "It must be the **fiercest** creature in the **world**," they said.

"Well, let's just hide here **quietly** and wait and see," said Owl **wisely**.

Finally, as the night fell, there was a **movement** from the cave and, much to everyone's **surprise**, out **crawled** a tiny, **scrawny caterpillar**.

Everyone was **speechless**, **except** for Owl.

"You may be small, but you are the **noisiest** of us all," he said with much **amusement**.

Spelling 3: Dictation test 3 (Book blurb)

Urgently, she took the **scissors**, cut the string and **unwrapped** the **parcel** of letters. Would they help her find the **Captain's** lost **treasure**? As she **removed** the contents, Sarah Jane sensed **trouble** ahead. Her **heart** began to beat faster.

And so begins the latest **fantastic** Sarah Jane **adventure**. In **easily** her **toughest** assignment yet, the **young** detective sets off on an **exciting** journey as she **searches** for **answers** to the many **questions**. But the clues are **misleading** and all is not what it seems …

Read on … you will not be **disappointed**.

From: **Spelling: Teacher's Resource Book** by Carol Matchett (ISBN 978 07217 1219 2). Copyright © Schofield & Sims Ltd, 2013. Published by Schofield & Sims Ltd, Dogley Mill, Fenay Bridge, Huddersfield HD8 0NQ, UK (www.schofieldandsims.co.uk). This page may be photocopied after purchase for use within your school or institution only.

Spelling 4: Dictation tests

The words omitted from the pupils' test sheet are those shown below in **bold**.

Spelling 4: Dictation test 1 (News report)

When **tomatoes** were stolen from the school garden, the children **decided** to tackle the matter **themselves**.

The young **gardeners** returned to the **scene** of the crime to keep **guard**. They were **sure** they could solve the **mystery**.

And soon they had **captured** the **thieves** on film – two grey squirrels!

The little **rogues** even **managed** to **gnaw** their way through the **special** netting.

The children have now set up a feeding **system** for the squirrels, to see **whether** that will help keep the plants safe. **They're certainly** hoping these two cheeky **characters** will stick to the peanuts in **future**.

Spelling 4: Dictation test 2 (Extract from myth)

In the **beginning**, there were no colours. Everything was **simply** a murky grey, just like **opaque** glass.

Land **disappeared** into sea; sea blended into sky. The animals were **almost invisible** against their **surroundings**.

Then one spring day, a little bird **discovered** a pot of colour. He **thought** he might **decorate** his feathers to **brighten** them up a bit. **Straight** away he **experimented** with a dab here and a flick of colour there. He was **delighted** with the results.

"I look **completely** different," he said, nodding with **approval**. "It's most **attractive**."

His new look caused great **excitement among** the other animals. Soon they all wanted some colour – and that was when the **quarrel** began.

Spelling 4: Dictation test 3 (Promotional material for charity)

Do you **realise** that your old **forgotten bicycle** could be a **valuable possession** for someone living in a remote part of Africa?

Obviously, your old **machine** might need a bit of work to make it **suitable** for the very **different** terrain of Africa. But once **redesigned** your **generous** gift can bring real **benefits** by

- helping **medical** workers reach villages
- helping children get to school to receive an **education**
- helping to **transport** people, water and goods
- helping **families** to start a **business**.

We are an **international** charity committed to **improving** the lives of others. Thank you for your **interest**.

Spelling 5: Dictation tests

The words omitted from the pupils' test sheet are those shown below in **bold**.

Spelling 5: Dictation test 1 (Guide to historic building)

The oldest parts of the castle date back to the **twelfth** century to the best of our **knowledge**. The part where you are standing is in an **extension** to the original castle. There is still some **rebuilding** going on following the **unfortunate** fire last year. This work is due for **completion** shortly.

Walk **through** the hall into the Yellow Drawing Room. This was Lady Jane's **favourite** room. Notice the high **ceilings** and tall elegant windows, which flood the room with **natural** light.

The library has many **unique** features. Note the fine tapestry on the wall **opposite** the fireplace, which gives the **impression** of grandeur.

The castle even has its own private **theatre**. Plays and masques were a **popular** form of entertainment in the seventeenth century and the family would have enjoyed **regular** performances.

Make sure you visit the dungeon before you leave. It is **believed** to be **haunted**. It is said that on cold winter nights the **deafening** cries of convicted **prisoners** can be heard coming from its damp walls.

Spelling 5: Dictation test 2 (Extract from traditional story)

The old soldier did not want to **deceive** the princesses, but he was **curious** to find out where they might be going.

Cautiously, he followed them across the lake to the **island** and down dimly lit tunnels.

Amazingly, the **journey** ended in a **magnificent** ballroom **illuminated** with thousands of tiny candles. Splendid **columns** covered in ivy rose to dizzying **heights**. The walls were studded with **precious** stones that **glistened** in the candlelight. **Several statues** stood guard around the room, so lifelike that the soldier wondered if they were **genuine** people turned to stone.

Musicians played merry tunes on their golden **instruments** as a mass of people danced to the lively **rhythm**.

It was **apparent** that no-one had noticed the **arrival** of the soldier amid all the **celebrations**.

Spelling 5: Dictation test 3 (Dialogue)

Teacher: Lucy, are you sure you locked the hamster cage?

Pupil: Yes, I **definitely** did. I filled the water bottle like I **usually** do and then …

Teacher: Yes, thank you, I am **familiar** with all that. I have no **doubt** it was entirely **accidental**, but really, Lucy, I do expect you to be more **reliable**. It's a **miracle** that we found Joey in the **corridor**. What if he'd got outside?

Pupil: I know and I'm **sincerely** sorry. I keep **imagining** poor Joey lost in the street, all alone.

Teacher: Well, yes, thank you Lucy. This is all most **regrettable**. There will have to be a **thorough investigation**, of course. In the meantime you are **forbidden** from going anywhere near the hamster cage.

Pupil: But Miss, that's **ridiculous**. On my **honour**, I …

Teacher: Don't **interrupt** … and there's no need for that **haughty** tone either. I can tell you Mrs Jenkins is **furious**. She can't believe you were so **irresponsible**.

From: **Spelling: Teacher's Resource Book** by Carol Matchett (ISBN 978 07217 1219 2). Copyright © Schofield & Sims Ltd, 2013. Published by Schofield & Sims Ltd, Dogley Mill, Fenay Bridge, Huddersfield HD8 0NQ, UK (www.schofieldandsims.co.uk). This page may be photocopied after purchase for use within your school or institution only.

Spelling 6: Dictation tests

The words omitted from the pupils' test sheet are those shown below in **bold**.

Spelling 6: Dictation test 1 (Extract from traditional story)

There was once an emperor who owned **enough** clothes to fill one hundred **wardrobes**.

One day two weavers arrived, demanding an **interview** with the Emperor.

"Tell his **Majesty** that we can **guarantee** him a suit that is **truly original**," said the **mischievous** weavers.

The weavers set about a **demonstration** of their skill. **Dramatically**, they set up their looms and began work – but with no threads.

"You see, to the **majority** of people there appears to be nothing there," they explained. "Only someone with your **wisdom** and **superior** taste can appreciate the **appearance** of this **particularly** fine material."

Of course the Emperor did not want to **embarrass** himself and seem **ignorant**. "Yes, yes," he blustered. "It is a miracle … simply **marvellous**. I'll take three suits."

"It is a **privilege** doing business with you," said the weavers, taking the Emperor's money but offering him no **receipt**.

Spelling 6: Dictation test 2 (Police report)

I was **patrolling** in the Green Lane area when I saw a man behaving in a **suspicious** manner. He was **noticeably** out of breath and seemed in a hurry.

At that moment a member of the public waved **frantically**, then **signalled** me to stop and asked for my **assistance**. I followed her into a nearby flat where there had clearly been some **disturbance**. I **immediately** requested backup as is normal **practice** in such cases.

The woman had a **minor** injury but further medical treatment was **unnecessary**. It seems she had returned home and **encountered** an **intruder**. The woman seemed **especially** concerned about a missing painting worth a **considerable** amount of money.

At this stage I updated my **colleagues** on **developments**. I **referred** them to the suspect in the street. I then returned to the **residence** to **re-examine** the scene.

Spelling 6: Dictation test 3 (Factual report on hurricanes)

Tropical storms go by a **variety** of names: hurricanes, **cyclones**, typhoons. They form high up in the **atmosphere**, usually beginning near the **equator** and then **travelling** across oceans, gaining force as they go. On reaching land, they have the **potential** to cause **tremendous** damage. The **effects** can be **disastrous**.

Radio warnings often **recommend** that people evacuate their homes, but not everyone takes the **advice**. Some choose to sit it out, **preferring** to stay in their boarded-up **properties**, frequently without **electricity**.

Those who do leave face days in temporary **accommodation** with just the bare **essentials**. And there is always the **possibility** of having no home to return to.

Read about one man's **miraculous** escape and how **technology** is helping weather forecasters to predict storms.

From: **Spelling: Teacher's Resource Book** by Carol Matchett (ISBN 978 07217 1219 2). Copyright © Schofield & Sims Ltd, 2013. Published by Schofield & Sims Ltd, Dogley Mill, Fenay Bridge, Huddersfield HD8 0NQ, UK (www.schofieldandsims.co.uk). This page may be photocopied after purchase for use within your school or institution only.

Spelling 1: Dictation test 1 – Response sheet

Name:	
Class:	Date:

**Your teacher will read this story. Write in the missing words.
Be sure to spell them correctly.**

I am a little _____ . I live in the _____ where I

_____ _____ . _____ see me

_____ _____ lily _____ or

_____ _____ the _____ .

I don't mind the _____ . I _____ _____

and race the _____ and _____ in their fun and

_____ .

Then, at _____ , I go to sleep _____ the

_____ .

Spelling 1: Dictation test 2 – Response sheet

Name:	
Class:	Date:

**Your teacher will read this story. Write in the missing words.
Be sure to spell them correctly.**

One _____, a big _____ _____ jumped

_____ out of the pan. It _____ _____ and

legs and _____ it ran.

A _____ _____ the _____ it met a little

_____. But she did not _____ it.

In the _____ it met two _____ but they did not stop and

_____ it.

Then it _____ to a _____.

"Jump on my _____," _____ a cunning fox. "I will

_____ you a lift."

But oh dear. Snip, snap went the fox. That was the end of that.

From: **Spelling: Teacher's Resource Book** by Carol Matchett (ISBN 978 07217 1219 2). Copyright © Schofield & Sims Ltd, 2013. Published by Schofield & Sims Ltd, Dogley Mill, Fenay Bridge, Huddersfield HD8 0NQ, UK (www.schofieldandsims.co.uk). This page may be photocopied after purchase for use within your school or institution only.

Spelling 1: Dictation test 3 – Response sheet

Name:	
Class:	Date:

**Your teacher will read this letter. Write in the missing words.
Be sure to spell them correctly.**

_____ Joe

Sorry you could not _____ to my _____

_____ on _____.

We _____ _____ _____ and ate on the

_____.

_____ it got _____ we went in and _____

musical _____ _____.

The _____ had _____ to _____ with.

Mum says you can _____ yours from my _____.

Best _____

From Shabnam

From: **Spelling: Teacher's Resource Book** by Carol Matchett (ISBN 978 07217 1219 2). Copyright © Schofield & Sims Ltd, 2013. Published by Schofield & Sims Ltd, Dogley Mill, Fenay Bridge, Huddersfield HD8 0NQ, UK (www.schofieldandsims.co.uk). This page may be photocopied after purchase for use within your school or institution only.

Spelling 2: Dictation test 1 – Response sheet

Name:	
Class:	Date:

Your teacher will read this description of a visit to a fairground. Write in the missing words. Be sure to spell them correctly.

"Are you _____ to go to the _____?"

_____ Dad.

Yes! We all _____ our hands and _____.

_____ a time we had! _____ _____ on the

big dipper, _____ down the helter-skelter, _____ from the

big _____. It was _____.

We _____ to _____ Dad on the _____

cars but it was no _____. He was too good.

There was just time to each have a _____

at _____ coconuts from the _____

_____ it was time to go.

From: **Spelling: Teacher's Resource Book** by Carol Matchett (ISBN 978 07217 1219 2). Copyright © Schofield & Sims Ltd, 2013. Published by Schofield & Sims Ltd, Dogley Mill, Fenay Bridge, Huddersfield HD8 0NQ, UK (www.schofieldandsims.co.uk).

Spelling 2: Dictation test 2 – Response sheet

Name:	
Class:	Date:

Your teacher will read this extract from a story. Write in the missing words. Be sure to spell them correctly.

Charlie the _____ _____ hid in the _____ of the tree.

He _____ a coconut on the lion as he _____ by.

"Whoops, _____ of me," said Charlie.

He _____ _____ at the leopard and her _____ sleeping _____.

"_____ out," said Charlie in a _____ sort of _____.

He _____ up his _____ banana to _____ at the _____.

But _____, Charlie's mum came up _____ Charlie.

"Charlie, you _____ not do that," she said.

From: **Spelling: Teacher's Resource Book** by Carol Matchett (ISBN 978 07217 1219 2). Copyright © Schofield & Sims Ltd, 2013. Published by Schofield & Sims Ltd, Dogley Mill, Fenay Bridge, Huddersfield HD8 0NQ, UK (www.schofieldandsims.co.uk). This page may be photocopied after purchase for use within your school or institution only.

Spelling 2: Dictation test 3 – Response sheet

Name:	
Class:	Date:

Your teacher will read this letter a child wrote about going to school. The child lived in Victorian times. Write in the missing words. Be sure to spell them correctly.

17th October 1894

Dear Harry

I thought you would like to hear about the _____ _____.

That is where I learn the _____ and I do this _____

_____. I keep a rag in my _____ so I can clean my

_____. The thing I like best is listening to _____.

There is a _____ in the _____ of the room so that is the

_____ place to sit in the _____.

The _____ are high up so we _____ see out.

Did I _____ the _____? She is _____.

Once my _____ of sums _____ her and she gave me a

_____.

Spelling 3: Dictation test 1 – Response sheet

Name:	
Class:	Date:

Your teacher will read this extract from a story. Write in the missing words. Be sure to spell them correctly.

The boy _____ over the wall and _____ down into the

_____ garden. Here the trees were as tall as _____ men.

_____ with _____ like velvet swayed in the breeze.

Raindrops _____ from the trees like a _____ ,

_____ in the now _____ _____ sunshine.

Rabbits _____ away as the boy _____ on the

_____ path. The _____ of birdsong _____ .

Even the insects _____ away and hid under _____ ,

_____ at this _____ .

Spelling 3: Dictation test 2 – Response sheet

Name:	
Class:	Date:

**Your teacher will read this traditional tale. Write in the missing words.
Be sure to spell them correctly.**

Who was hiding in the cave?

"Stay away or I will _____ you to dust," warned a _____

voice from inside the cave.

When they _____ that, all the other _____

_____.

The mice began the _____. "It must be the _____ creature

in the _____," they said.

"Well, let's just hide here _____ and wait and see," said Owl

_____.

_____, as the night fell, there was a _____ from the

cave and, much to everyone's _____, out _____ a tiny,

_____ _____.

Everyone was _____, _____ for Owl.

"You may be small, but you are the _____ of us all,"

he said with much _____.

*From: **Spelling: Teacher's Resource Book** by Carol Matchett (ISBN 978 07217 1219 2). Copyright © Schofield & Sims Ltd, 2013. Published by Schofield & Sims Ltd, Dogley Mill, Fenay Bridge, Huddersfield HD8 0NQ, UK (www.schofieldandsims.co.uk). This page may be photocopied after purchase for use within your school or institution only.*

Spelling 3: Dictation test 3 – Response sheet

Name:	
Class:	Date:

Your teacher will read this blurb for a new book in a series. Write in the missing words. Be sure to spell them correctly.

_____, she took the _____, cut the string and

_____ the _____ of letters. Would they help her find the

_____ lost _____? As she _____ the

contents, Sarah Jane sensed _____ ahead. Her _____

began to beat faster.

And so begins the latest _____ Sarah Jane _____.

In _____ her _____ assignment yet, the

_____ detective sets off on an _____ journey as she

_____ for _____ to the many _____.

But the clues are _____ and all is not what it seems ...

Read on ... you will not be _____.

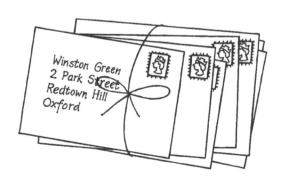

Winston Green
2 Park Street
Redtown Hill
Oxford

From: **Spelling: Teacher's Resource Book** by Carol Matchett (ISBN 978 07217 1219 2). Copyright © Schofield & Sims Ltd, 2013. Published by Schofield & Sims Ltd, Dogley Mill, Fenay Bridge, Huddersfield HD8 0NQ, UK (www.schofieldandsims.co.uk). This page may be photocopied after purchase for use within your school or institution only.

Spelling 4: Dictation test 1 – Response sheet

Name:	
Class:	Date:

Your teacher will read this local news report. Write in the missing words. Be sure to spell them correctly.

When _____ were stolen from the school garden, the children

_____ to tackle the matter _____ .

The young _____ returned to the _____ of the crime

to keep _____ . They were _____ they could solve the

_____ .

And soon they had _____ the _____ on film – two grey

squirrels!

The little _____ even _____ to _____ their

way through the _____ netting.

The children have now set up a feeding _____ for the squirrels, to see

_____ that will help keep the plants safe.

_____ _____ hoping these

two cheeky _____ will stick to the peanuts

in _____ .

Spelling 4: Dictation test 2 – Response sheet

Name:	
Class:	Date:

Your teacher will read this extract from a myth. Write in the missing words. Be sure to spell them correctly.

In the _____, there were no colours. Everything was _____

a murky grey, just like _____ glass.

Land _____ into sea; sea blended into sky. The animals were

_____ _____ against their _____.

Then one spring day, a little bird _____ a pot of colour.

He _____ he might _____ his feathers

to _____ them up a bit. _____ away he

_____ with a dab here and a flick of colour there. He was

_____ with the results.

"I look _____ different," he said, nodding with _____.

"It's most _____."

His new look caused great _____

_____ the other animals. Soon

they all wanted some colour – and that was

when the _____ began.

From: **Spelling: Teacher's Resource Book** by Carol Matchett (ISBN 978 07217 1219 2). Copyright © Schofield & Sims Ltd, 2013. Published by Schofield & Sims Ltd, Dogley Mill, Fenay Bridge, Huddersfield HD8 0NQ, UK (www.schofieldandsims.co.uk). This page may be photocopied after purchase for use within your school or institution only.

Spelling 4: Dictation test 3 – Response sheet

Name:	
Class:	Date:

Your teacher will read this appeal from a charity. Write in the missing words. Be sure to spell them correctly.

Do you _____ that your old _____ _____ could be a _____ _____ for someone living in a remote part of Africa?

_____, your old _____ might need a bit of work to make it _____ for the very _____ terrain of Africa. But once _____ your _____ gift can bring real _____ by

• helping _____ workers reach villages

• helping children get to school to receive an _____

• helping to _____ people, water and goods

• helping _____ to start a _____.

We are an _____ charity committed to _____ the lives of others.

Thank you for your _____.

*From: **Spelling: Teacher's Resource Book** by Carol Matchett (ISBN 978 07217 1219 2). Copyright © Schofield & Sims Ltd, 2013. Published by Schofield & Sims Ltd, Dogley Mill, Fenay Bridge, Huddersfield HD8 0NQ, UK (www.schofieldandsims.co.uk). This page may be photocopied after purchase for use within your school or institution only.*

Spelling 5: Dictation test 1 – Response sheet

Name:	
Class:	Date:

**Your teacher will read this guide to a castle. Write in the missing words.
Be sure to spell them correctly.**

The oldest parts of the castle date back to the _____ century to the best of

our _____. The part where you are standing is in an _____

to the original castle. There is still some _____ going on following the

_____ fire last year. This work is due for _____ shortly.

Walk _____ the hall into the Yellow Drawing Room. This was Lady Jane's

_____ room. Notice the high _____ and tall elegant

windows, which flood the room with _____ light.

The library has many _____ features. Note the fine tapestry on the wall

_____ the fireplace, which gives the _____ of grandeur.

The castle even has its own private _____. Plays and masques were a

_____ form of entertainment in the seventeenth century and the family

would have enjoyed _____ performances.

Make sure you visit the dungeon before you leave. It is _____

to be _____. It is said that on cold winter nights

the _____ cries of convicted _____

can be heard coming from its damp walls.

*From: **Spelling: Teacher's Resource Book** by Carol Matchett (ISBN 978 07217 1219 2). Copyright © Schofield & Sims Ltd, 2013. Published by Schofield & Sims Ltd, Dogley Mill,
Fenay Bridge, Huddersfield HD8 0NQ, UK (www.schofieldandsims.co.uk). This page may be photocopied after purchase for use within your school or institution only.*

Spelling 5: Dictation test 2 – Response sheet

Name:	
Class:	Date:

Your teacher will read this extract from a traditional story. Write in the missing words. Be sure to spell them correctly.

The old soldier did not want to _____ the princesses, but he was

_____ to find out where they might be going.

_____, he followed them across the lake to the _____ and

down dimly lit tunnels.

Amazingly, the _____ ended in a _____ ballroom

_____ with thousands of tiny candles. Splendid _____

covered in ivy rose to dizzying _____. The walls were studded

with _____ stones that _____ in the candlelight.

_____ _____ stood guard around the room, so lifelike that

the soldier wondered if they were _____ people turned to stone.

_____ played merry tunes on their golden _____ as a mass

of people danced to the lively _____.

It was _____ that no-one had noticed

the _____ of the soldier amid all the

_____.

From: **Spelling: Teacher's Resource Book** by Carol Matchett (ISBN 978 07217 1219 2). Copyright © Schofield & Sims Ltd, 2013. Published by Schofield & Sims Ltd, Dogley Mill, Fenay Bridge, Huddersfield HD8 0NQ, UK (www.schofieldandsims.co.uk). This page may be photocopied after purchase for use within your school or institution only.

Spelling 5: Dictation test 3 – Response sheet

Name:	
Class:	Date:

Your teacher will read this dialogue between teacher and pupil. Write in the missing words. Be sure to spell them correctly.

Teacher: Lucy, are you sure you locked the hamster cage?

Pupil: Yes, I _____ did. I filled the water bottle like I _____

do and then ...

Teacher: Yes, thank you, I am _____ with all that. I have no

_____ it was entirely _____, but really, Lucy, I do expect

you to be more _____. It's a _____ that we found Joey in

the _____. What if he'd got outside?

Pupil: I know and I'm _____ sorry. I keep _____ poor Joey

lost in the street, all alone.

Teacher: Well, yes, thank you Lucy. This is all most _____. There will have

to be a _____ _____, of course. In the meantime you are

_____ from going anywhere near the hamster cage.

Pupil: But Miss, that's _____. On my _____, I ...

Teacher: Don't _____ ... and there's no need for that _____

tone either. I can tell you Mrs Jenkins is _____. She can't believe you were

so _____.

From: **Spelling: Teacher's Resource Book** by Carol Matchett (ISBN 978 07217 1219 2). Copyright © Schofield & Sims Ltd, 2013. Published by Schofield & Sims Ltd, Dogley Mill, Fenay Bridge, Huddersfield HD8 0NQ, UK (www.schofieldandsims.co.uk). This page may be photocopied after purchase for use within your school or institution only.

Spelling 6: Dictation test 1 – Response sheet

Name:	
Class:	Date:

Your teacher will read this extract from a traditional story. Write in the missing words. Be sure to spell them correctly.

There was once an emperor who owned _____ clothes to fill one hundred

_____.

One day two weavers arrived, demanding an _____ with the Emperor.

"Tell his _____ that we can _____ him a suit that is

_____ _____," said the _____ weavers.

The weavers set about a _____ of their skill. _____, they

set up their looms and began work – but with no threads.

"You see, to the _____ of people there appears to be nothing there," they

explained. "Only someone with your _____ and _____

taste can appreciate the _____ of this _____ fine material."

Of course the Emperor did not want to _____ himself and seem

_____. "Yes, yes," he blustered. "It is a miracle ... simply

_____. I'll take three suits."

"It is a _____ doing business with you," said the weavers, taking the

Emperor's money but offering him no _____.

From: **Spelling: Teacher's Resource Book** by Carol Matchett (ISBN 978 07217 1219 2). Copyright © Schofield & Sims Ltd, 2013. Published by Schofield & Sims Ltd, Dogley Mill,
Fenay Bridge, Huddersfield HD8 0NQ, UK (www.schofieldandsims.co.uk). This page may be photocopied after purchase for use within your school or institution only.

Spelling 6: Dictation test 2 – Response sheet

Name:	
Class:	Date:

Your teacher will read this police report. Write in the missing words. Be sure to spell them correctly.

I was _____ in the Green Lane area when I saw a man behaving in a _____ manner. He was _____ out of breath and seemed in a hurry.

At that moment a member of the public waved _____, then _____ me to stop and asked for my _____. I followed her into a nearby flat where there had clearly been some _____. I _____ requested backup as is normal _____ in such cases.

The woman had a _____ injury but further medical treatment was _____. It seems she had returned home and _____ an _____. The woman seemed _____ concerned about a missing painting worth a _____ amount of money.

At this stage I updated my _____ on _____. I _____ them to the suspect in the street. I then returned to the _____ to _____ the scene.

From: Spelling: Teacher's Resource Book by Carol Matchett (ISBN 978 07217 1219 2). Copyright © Schofield & Sims Ltd, 2013. Published by Schofield & Sims Ltd, Dogley Mill, Fenay Bridge, Huddersfield HD8 0NQ, UK (www.schofieldandsims.co.uk). This page may be photocopied after purchase for use within your school or institution only.

Spelling 6: Dictation test 3 – Response sheet

Name:	
Class:	Date:

Your teacher will read this information about hurricanes. Write in the missing words. Be sure to spell them correctly.

_____ storms go by a _____ of names: hurricanes,

_____, typhoons. They form high up in the _____, usually

beginning near the _____ and then _____ across oceans,

gaining force as they go. On reaching land, they have the _____ to cause

_____ damage. The _____ can be _____.

Radio warnings often _____ that people evacuate their homes,

but not everyone takes the _____. Some choose to sit it out,

_____ to stay in their boarded-up _____, frequently

without _____.

Those who do leave face days in temporary _____ with just the bare

_____. And there is always the _____ of having no home

to return to.

Read about one man's _____ escape and how _____ is

helping weather forecasters to predict storms.

From: **Spelling: Teacher's Resource Book** by Carol Matchett (ISBN 978 07217 1219 2). Copyright © Schofield & Sims Ltd, 2013. Published by Schofield & Sims Ltd, Dogley Mill, Fenay Bridge, Huddersfield HD8 0NQ, UK (www.schofieldandsims.co.uk). This page may be photocopied after purchase for use within your school or institution only.

Dictation assessment sheet

| Name: |
| Class: |

Dictation 1 _____   Date _____

_____

Dictation 2 _____   Date _____

_____

Dictation 3 _____   Date _____

_____

Dictation 4 _____   Date _____

_____

Dictation 5 _____   Date _____

_____

Spelling 1: Test 1 – Error analysis sheet

Teacher's name:							
Class:						Date:	

Word	Focus	Pupils' names						Total errors per focus
frog	ccvc word **fr**							
pond	cvcc word **nd**							
was	tricky word							
born	vowel digraph **or**							
you	tricky word							
jumping	adding **ing**							
off	word ending **ff**							
pads	cvc word							
	adding **s** to plurals							
playing	vowel digraph **ay**							
	adding **ing**							
with	consonant digraph **th**							
ducks	word ending **ck**							
	adding **s** to plurals							
rain	vowel digraph **ai**							
still	ccvc word **st**							
	word ending **ll**							
swim	ccvc word **sw**							
fish	consonant digraph **sh**							
join	vowel digraph **oi**							
games	vowel digraph **a-e**							
	adding **s** to plurals							
sunset	compound word							
	cvc words							
under	two-syllable word							
	word ending **er**							
stars	vowel digraph **ar**							
	adding **s** to plurals							
Total errors per pupil								

Spelling 1: Test 2 – Error analysis sheet

Teacher's name:		
Class:	Date:	

Word	Focus	Pupils' names							Total errors per focus
morning	vowel digraph **or**								
	two syllables (/**ing**)								
round	vowel digraph **ou**								
	consonant cluster (blend **nd**)								
pancake	compound word								
	vowel digraph **a-e**								
right	vowel trigraph **igh**								
grew	consonant cluster (blend **gr**)								
	vowel digraph **ew**								
arms	vowel digraph **ar**								
	add **s** to plurals								
away	vowel digraph **ay**								
mile	vowel digraph **i-e**								
down	vowel digraph **ow**								
road	vowel digraph **oa**								
girl	vowel digraph **ir**								
catch	word ending **tch**								
farmyard	compound word								
	vowel digraph **ar**								
sheep	consonant digraph **sh**								
	vowel digraph **ee**								
eat	vowel digraph **ea**								
came	vowel digraph **a-e**								
river	two syllables								
	word ending **er**								
nose	vowel digraph **o-e**								
said	tricky word								
give	word ending **ve**								
Total errors per pupil									

From: **Spelling: Teacher's Resource Book** by Carol Matchett (ISBN 978 07217 1219 2). Copyright © Schofield & Sims Ltd, 2013. Published by Schofield & Sims Ltd, Dogley Mill, Fenay Bridge, Huddersfield HD8 0NQ, UK (www.schofieldandsims.co.uk). This page may be photocopied after purchase for use within your school or institution only.

Spelling 1: Test 3 – Error analysis sheet

Teacher's name:							
Class:						Date:	

Word	Focus	Pupils' names						Total errors per focus
dear	vowel trigraph **ear**							
come	tricky word							
birthday	vowel digraph **ir**							
	compound word							
party	vowel digraph **ar**							
	word ending **y**							
Thursday	vowel digraph **ur**							
	day of week							
played	vowel digraph **ay**							
	adding **ed** to verbs							
football	compound word							
	vowel digraph **oo** ('u')							
	tricky word (**all**)							
outside	compound word							
	vowel digraph **ou**							
	vowel digraph **i-e**							
benches	word ending **nch**							
	adding **es** to plural							
when	**wh** spelling							
colder	**old** spelling							
	adding **er**							
enjoyed	vowel digraph **oy**							
	two syllables (**en/joy**)							
	adding **ed** to verb							
chairs	consonant digraph **ch**							
	vowel trigraph **air**							
	adding **s** to plurals							
instead	two syllables (**in/stead**)							
	vowel digraph **ea** ('e')							
children	consonant digraph **ch**							
	two syllables (**dren**)							
stickers	ccvc, **ck** ending (**stick**)							
	adding **er**							
	adding **s** to plurals							
leave	vowel digraph **ea**							
	word ending **ve**							
fetch	word ending **tch**							
house	vowel digraph **ou**							
	word ending **se**							
wishes	consonant digraph **sh**							
	adding **es** to plurals							
Total errors per pupil								

Spelling 2: Test 1 – Error analysis sheet

Teacher's name:		
Class:		Date:

Word	Focus	Pupils' names						Total errors per focus
ready	**ea** digraph ('e')							
	y ending ('ee')							
fairground	compound word							
	trigraph **air**							
	vowel digraph **ou**							
asked	**sk**							
	adding **ed** ('t' sound)							
clapped	adding **ed** (double consonant)							
cheered	**eer** spelling of 'ear'							
	adding **ed**							
what	**wh**							
	w special **a** ('o')							
shooting	vowel digraph **oo**							
	adding **ing**							
along	**o** spelling							
sliding	split digraph **i-e**							
	adding **ing** (drop **e**)							
waving	split digraph **a-e**							
	add **ing** (drop **e**)							
wheel	**wh**							
	vowel digraph **ee**							
great	tricky word (**ea** spelling of 'a-e')							
tried	adding **ed** (**y** to **i**)							
dodge	**dge**							
bumper	consonant cluster (blend **mp**)							
	adding **er**							
use	**u-e** spelling of '(y)oo'							
turn	vowel digraph **ur**							
knocking	**kn** spelling of 'n'							
	ck							
	adding **ing**							
shy	**y** spelling of 'i-e' at end of words							
before	**ore** spelling of 'or'							
Total errors per pupil								

Spelling 2: Test 2 – Error analysis sheet

Teacher's name:							
Class:					Date:		

Word	Focus	Pupils' names						Total errors per focus
cheeky	vowel digraph **ee**							
	adding **y**							
monkey	'u' sound spelt **o**							
	'ee' sound spelt **ey**							
branches	consonant clusters							
	adding **es**							
dropped	adding **ed** (doubling final consonant)							
walked	**al** spelling of 'aw'							
	adding **ed** ('t')							
careless	vowel trigraph **are**							
	adding suffix **less**							
squirted	**squ**							
	vowel digraph **ir**							
	adding **ed** ('id')							
water	tricky word (**wa**)							
	er							
babies	tricky word							
	adding **es** (**y** to **i**)							
nearby	compound word							
	vowel graphemes							
watch	**wa** spelling of 'wo'							
	tch							
helpful	cvcc							
	adding suffix **ful**							
voice	vowel digraph **oi**							
	ce spelling of 's'							
squashed	**squ**							
	a spelling of 'o'							
	adding **ed**							
ripest	vowel digraph **i-e**							
	adding suffix **est**							
	drop **e**							
throw	**thr**							
	vowel digraph **ow**							
giraffe	**g** spelling of 'j'							
	vowel digraph **ir**							
	tricky word (**affe**)							
meanwhile	compound word							
	vowel digraphs							
	wh							
behind	compound word							
	i spelling of 'i-e'							
should	tricky word							
Total errors per pupil								

Spelling 2: Test 3 – Error analysis sheet

Teacher's name:							
Class:						Date:	

Word	Focus	Pupils' names						Total errors per focus
village	two syllables							
	ge ending (**ge** spelling of 'j')							
school	tricky word							
	ch spelling of 'k'							
	vowel digraph **oo**							
alphabet	three-syllable word							
	ph spelling of 'f'							
fancy	**c** spelling of 's'							
	y spelling of 'ee'							
handwriting	compound word							
	wr spelling of 'r'							
	adding **ing** (drop **e**)							
pocket	two-syllable word							
	ck							
	et ending							
slate	consonant blend							
	vowel digraph **a-e**							
stories	adding **es** (**y** to **i**)							
stove	consonant blend							
	vowel digraph **o-e**							
middle	two-syllable word							
	le ending							
warmest	tricky word (**warm**)							
	adding suffix **est**							
winter	two-syllable word							
	er ending							
windows	two-syllable word							
	ow ending							
	adding **s**							
can't	contraction							
mention	two-syllable word							
	tion ending							
teacher	vowel digraph **ea**							
	adding suffix **er**							
scary	vowel trigraph **are**							
	adding **y** (drop **e**)							
page	vowel digraph **a-e**							
	g spelling of 'j'							
displeased	vowel digraph **ea**							
	prefix **dis**							
	adding **ed**							
caning	vowel digraph **a-e**							
	adding **ing** (drop **e**)							
Total errors per pupil								

From: *Spelling: Teacher's Resource Book* by Carol Matchett (ISBN 978 07217 1219 2). Copyright © Schofield & Sims Ltd, 2013. Published by Schofield & Sims Ltd, Dogley Mill, Fenay Bridge, Huddersfield HD8 0NQ, UK (www.schofieldandsims.co.uk). This page may be photocopied after purchase for use within your school or institution only.

Spelling 3: Test 1 – Error analysis sheet

Teacher's name:							
Class:						Date:	

Word	Focus	Pupils' names						Total errors per focus
climbed	silent **b**							
	adding **ed**							
scrambled	**le** ending							
	adding **ed**							
hidden	doubling consonant							
	adding **en**							
eight	tricky word							
	eigh = 'ai' sound							
poppies	double consonant (**y**)							
	adding **es** (**y** to **i**)							
petals	**al** ending							
	adding **s**							
tumbled	**le** ending							
	adding **ed**							
fountain	vowel digraph **ou**							
	ain ending							
sparkling	**le** ending							
	adding **ing**							
brilliant	double consonant							
	ant ending							
August	tricky word (**au** and month of year)							
scurried	double **r**							
	adding **ed** (**y** to **i**)							
stepped	adding **ed** (double consonant)							
stony	root word **stone**							
	adding **y** (drop **e**)							
chorus	**ch** spelling of 'k'							
	two-syllable word							
faded	root word **fade**							
	adding **ed** (drop **e**)							
wriggled	**wr** spelling of 'r'							
	double consonant							
	adding **ed** to **le**							
daisies	vowel digraph **ai**							
	adding **es** (**y** to **i**)							
staring	vowel trigraph **are**							
	adding **ing**							
stranger	**g** spelling of 'j'							
	er ending							
Total errors per pupil								

Spelling 3: Test 2 – Error analysis sheet

Teacher's name:

Class: | **Date:**

Word	Focus	Pupils' names						Total errors per focus
trample	two syllables							
	le ending							
fearful	vowel trigraph **ear**							
	ful suffix							
heard	tricky word (**ear**)							
	homophone							
animals	syllables							
	al ending							
	plural							
trembled	**le** ending							
	adding **ed**							
panic	**ic** ending							
fiercest	tricky vowel (**ier**)							
	ce							
	adding **est**							
world	**w** special (**wor**)							
	ld ending							
quietly	tricky word **quiet**							
	adding **ly**							
wisely	**ise**							
	adding **ly**							
finally	**al** ending							
	adding **ly**							
movement	spelling of 'oo'							
	ment suffix							
surprise	spelling of 'er'							
	prise							
crawled	vowel digraph **aw**							
	adding **ed**							
scrawny	vowel digraph **aw**							
	adding **y**							
caterpillar	syllables							
	er/ar							
speechless	vowel grapheme							
	adding **less**							
except	**ex**							
	soft **c**							
noisiest	root word **noisy**							
	adding **est** (**y** to **i**)							
amusement	vowel digraph **u-e**							
	ment suffix							
Total errors per pupil								

From: *Spelling: Teacher's Resource Book* by Carol Matchett (ISBN 978 07217 1219 2). Copyright © Schofield & Sims Ltd, 2013. Published by Schofield & Sims Ltd, Dogley Mill, Fenay Bridge, Huddersfield HD8 0NQ, UK (www.schofieldandsims.co.uk). This page may be photocopied after purchase for use within your school or institution only.

Spelling 3: Test 3 – Error analysis sheet

Teacher's name:		
Class:		Date:

Word	Focus	Pupils' names						Total errors per focus
urgently	vowel digraph **ur**							
	soft **g**							
	adding **ly**							
scissors	**sc** (silent **c**)							
	or(**s**) ending							
unwrapped	**un** prefix							
	wr spelling of 'r'							
	adding **ed** (double consonant)							
parcel	soft **c**							
	el ending							
captain's	**ain** ending							
	possessive apostrophe							
treasure	**ea**							
	sure ending							
removed	**re** prefix							
	o-e ('oo')							
	adding **ed**							
trouble	**ou** spelling of 'u'							
	le ending							
heart	tricky word (**ear**)							
fantastic	syllables							
	ic ending							
adventure	syllables							
	ture ending							
easily	**eas**							
	adding **ly** (**ily**)							
toughest	tricky word (**ough**)							
	adding **est**							
young	tricky word							
	ou spelling of 'u'							
exciting	**ex**							
	soft **c**							
	adding **ing**							
searches	**ear** spelling of 'er'							
	adding **es**							
answers	silent **w**							
	ers							
questions	**qu**							
	tion ending							
misleading	**mis** prefix							
disappointed	**dis** prefix							
	double **p**							
	adding **ed**							
Total errors per pupil								

Spelling 4: Test 1 – Error analysis sheet

Teacher's name:		
Class:		Date:

Word	Focus	Pupils' names						Total errors per focus
tomatoes	word ending **o**							
	plural – adding **es**							
decided	soft **c**							
	adding **ed**							
themselves	compound word							
	plural **ves**							
gardeners	syllables							
	adding **er/s**							
scene	homophone							
	sc spelling of 's'							
guard	**gu** spelling of 'g'							
sure	tricky word							
mystery	**y** spelling of 'i'							
	syllables (**ster/y**)							
captured	**ture** ending							
	adding **ed**							
thieves	vowel digraph **ie**							
	plural **ves**							
rogues	**gue** ending ('g')							
	adding **s**							
managed	**age** second syllable							
	adding **ed**							
gnaw	**gn** spelling of 'n'							
	vowel digraph **aw**							
special	tricky word							
system	**y** spelling of 'i'							
	second syllable							
whether	homophone							
	wh							
they're	homophone							
	apostrophe							
certainly	soft **c**							
	syllables							
	suffix **ly**							
characters	**ch** spelling of 'k'							
	syllables							
future	**ture** ending							
Total errors per pupil								

Spelling 4: Test 2 – Error analysis sheet

Teacher's name:							
Class:						Date:	

Word	Focus	Pupils' names						Total errors per focus
beginning	syllables							
	adding **ing** (doubling consonant)							
simply	suffix **ly**							
	word ending **le**							
opaque	**que** ending ('k' sound)							
disappeared	adding prefix **dis**							
	ap/pear							
	adding **ed**							
almost	prefix **al**							
invisible	prefix **in**							
	ible ending							
surroundings	prefix **sur**							
	building word (adding prefix/suffix)							
discovered	prefix **dis**							
	adding **ed**							
thought	**ough** letter string							
decorate	syllables							
	c spelling of 'k'							
	suffix **ate**							
brighten	**ight** letter string							
	adding **en**							
straight	**aight** letter string							
experimented	syllables							
	ex							
	adding **ed**							
delighted	prefix **de**							
	adding **ed**							
completely	**com/plete**							
	adding **ly** (keep **e**)							
approval	**ap/prove**							
	adding **al** (drop **e**)							
attractive	**at/tract**							
	adding **ive**							
excitement	root word **ex/cite**							
	adding **ment** (keep **e**)							
among	prefix **a**							
	o spelling of 'u'							
quarrel	**qua** (**a** spelling of 'o')							
	double consonant **rr**							
	(rr)el							
Total errors per pupil								

Spelling 4: Test 3 – Error analysis sheet

Teacher's name:

Class: | Date:

Word	Focus	Pupils' names						Total errors per focus
realise	root word **real**							
	suffix **ise**							
forgotten	adding **en**							
	double consonant							
bicycle	root **bi**							
	cycle							
valuable	root word **value**							
	suffix **able**							
	drop **e**							
possession	**ssion** spelling of 'shun'							
	root word **possess**							
obviously	**ious** ending							
	suffix **ly**							
machine	**ch** spelling of 'sh'							
	ine							
suitable	**ui** spelling of 'oo'							
	suffix **able**							
different	syllables (**fer** unstressed)							
	double **f**							
	ent ending							
redesigned	root word **sign**							
	adding affixes							
generous	soft **g**							
	unstressed syllable (**er**)							
	ous ending							
benefits	unstressed middle vowel							
medical	**med-ic**							
	suffix **al**							
education	suffix **ation**							
transport	roots **trans/port**							
families	unstressed **i**							
	plural (**y** to **ies**)							
business	root word **busy**							
	suffix **ness**							
	y to 'i'							
international	**inter**							
	nation							
	suffix **al**							
improving	**im/prove**							
	adding **ing** (drop **e**)							
interest	syllables (unstressed **er**)							
Total errors per pupil								

Spelling 5: Test 1 – Error analysis sheet

Teacher's name:		
Class:	Date:	

Word	Focus	Pupils' names						Total errors per focus
twelfth	tricky word – unstressed consonant							
knowledge	root word **know**							
	unstressed **e**							
extension	**sion** spelling of 'shun'							
rebuilding	root word **build**							
	adding affixes							
unfortunate	root word **fortune**							
	adding affixes							
	drop **e** to add **ate**							
completion	root word **complete**							
	(t)ion suffix							
through	**ough** letter string							
favourite	**our** letter string							
	ite ending							
ceilings	soft **c**							
	'ee' spelt **ei** after **c**							
natural	unstressed vowels							
	natur(e)							
	al suffix							
unique	**uni**							
	que spelling of 'k'							
opposite	tricky word							
	unstressed vowel							
impression	**ssion** ('shun')							
	im/press							
theatre	**ea** letter string							
	re ending							
popular	unstressed vowels							
regular	unstressed vowels							
believed	**ie** spelling ('ee')							
	adding **ed**							
haunted	**au** letter string							
deafening	unstressed middle syllable							
prisoners	unstressed **o**							
	er ending							
Total errors per pupil								

Spelling 5: Test 2 – Error analysis sheet

Teacher's name:							
Class:					Date:		

Word	Focus	Pupils' names						Total errors per focus
deceive	**c** spelling of 's'							
	'ee' spelt **ei** after **c**							
curious	**cu** = 'q' sound							
	ious ending							
cautiously	**au** pattern							
	tious ('shus') ending							
	ly suffix							
island	silent letter							
journey	tricky word (**our** letter string)							
magnificent	syllables							
	c spelling of 's' (**ce**)							
	ent ending							
illuminated	**il** prefix (**ill**)							
	syllables							
	u spelling of 'oo' sound (**lum**)							
columns	silent letter							
heights	**eigh** letter string							
precious	**cious** ('shus') ending							
glistened	silent **t**							
	unstressed vowels							
several	unstressed vowels							
statues	**tue** ('chew')							
genuine	**g** spelling of 'j' (**ge**)							
	ine ending							
musicians	root word **music**							
	cian spelling of 'shun'							
instruments	unstressed vowel **u**							
	ment suffix							
rhythm	silent letter (**rh**)							
	y spelling of 'i'							
	consonant cluster **thm**							
apparent	**ap** prefix (**app**)							
	single **r**							
	ent ending							
arrival	**ar** prefix (**arr**)							
	adding **al** (drop **e**)							
celebrations	**c** spelling of 's' (**ce**)							
	unstressed vowel							
	adding **tion**							
Total errors per pupil								

From: **Spelling: Teacher's Resource Book** by Carol Matchett (ISBN 978 07217 1219 2). Copyright © Schofield & Sims Ltd, 2013. Published by Schofield & Sims Ltd, Dogley Mill, Fenay Bridge, Huddersfield HD8 0NQ, UK (www.schofieldandsims.co.uk). This page may be photocopied after purchase for use within your school or institution only.

Schofield & Sims Spelling

Spelling 5: Test 3 – Error analysis sheet

Teacher's name:

Class: | Date:

Word	Focus	Pupils' names						Total errors per focus
definitely	unstressed vowels							
	adding **ly** (keep **e**)							
usually	tricky word **usual**							
	ly suffix							
familiar	unstressed vowels							
doubt	silent letter **bt**							
accidental	letter **c** sounds 'ac/ci'							
	al suffix							
	unstressed vowels							
reliable	**rely** – y to i							
	able ending							
miracle	unstressed ending **acle**							
corridor	double **r**							
	or ending							
sincerely	**c** spelling of 's' (**ce**)							
	ere							
	adding **ly** (keep **e**)							
imagining	**g** spelling of 'j' (**gi**)							
	adding **ing** (drop **e**)							
regrettable	**able** ending							
	double **t**							
thorough	**ough** letter string							
	tho							
investigation	**in/ve/sti/gate**							
	ation ending							
forbidden	**en** ending							
	forbid (double **dd** to add **en**)							
ridiculous	**ous** ending							
	adding to **ridicule** (drop the **e**)							
honour	**our** letter string							
	silent **h**							
interrupt	**inter** prefix							
	double **r**							
haughty	**augh** letter string							
	y ending							
furious	**ous** ending							
	fury – y to i							
irresponsible	**ir** prefix (**ir/re**)							
	response							
	ible (drop **e**)							
Total errors per pupil								

Spelling 6: Test 1 – Error analysis sheet

Teacher's name:							
Class:						Date:	

Word	Focus	Pupils' names						Total errors per focus
enough	**ough** letter string							
wardrobes	**(w)ar** spelling of 'or'							
interview	**inter** prefix							
	view							
majesty	unstressed vowel							
	link to **majestic**							
guarantee	**gu** spelling of 'g'							
	unstressed vowel							
truly	**ly** suffix (exception)							
original	unstressed vowel							
	origin + al							
	g spelling of 'j' (**gi**)							
mischievous	**mischief** (v)							
	ous ending							
demonstration	syllables							
	adding **ation**							
dramatically	**dramatic** (**ic**)							
	ly suffix (**ally** not **ly**)							
majority	**major** (**or** ending)							
	adding **ity**							
wisdom	link to **wise**							
	dom ending							
superior	link to **super**							
	ior ending							
appearance	**ap/pear**							
	ance ending							
particularly	unstressed consonant (link to **part**)							
	cu = 'q' sound							
	ar ending							
	ly suffix							
embarrass	double letters							
ignorant	unstressed vowel (link to **ignore**)							
	ant ending							
marvellous	link to **marvel**							
	ous ending							
	double final **l**							
privilege	unstressed vowels							
receipt	**c** spelling of 's'							
	'ee' spelt **ei** after **c**							
	silent letter **p**							
Total errors per pupil								

Spelling 6: Test 2 – Error analysis sheet

Teacher's name:		
Class:	Date:	

Word	Focus	Pupils' names						Total errors per focus
patrolling	ol							
	+ **ing** to **l** = **lling**							
suspicious	**cious** spelling of 'shus'							
noticeably	**c** spelling of 's'							
	keep **e** to add **able**							
	ly suffix (**ably**)							
frantically	**fran/tic** (**ic**)							
	ly suffix (**ally**)							
signalled	**al**							
	+ **ed** to **l** = **lled**							
assistance	**as/sist**							
	ance ending							
disturbance	**dis/turb**							
	ance ending							
immediately	double letter **im/m**							
	unstressed vowel							
	keep **e** to add **ly**							
practice	**ce/se** confusion							
minor	homophone							
	or ending							
unnecessary	**un/n** prefix							
	single **c**, double **ss**							
	ary ending							
encountered	**en** prefix							
	er + **ed**							
intruder	**u-e** spelling of 'oo'							
	adding **er**							
especially	**e** prefix							
	cial spelling 'shul'							
	ly prefix (**lly**)							
considerable	unstressed syllable (**er**)							
	able ending							
colleagues	**col/l**							
	gue spelling of 'g'							
developments	unstressed vowel							
	ment suffix							
referred	stressed **fer**							
	double **r** to add **ed**							
residence	**ence** ending							
re-examine	hyphen with prefix							
	ex/am							
Total errors per pupil								

Spelling 6: Test 3 – Error analysis sheet

Teacher's name:							
Class:					Date:		

Word	Focus	Pupils' names						Total errors per focus
tropical	ic							
	+ al							
variety	root **var(y)** (y to i)							
	+ ety							
cyclones	cy (link to cycle)							
atmosphere	roots atmo/sphere							
equator	equat(e)							
	or ending							
travelling	el ending							
	+ ing to el = lling							
potential	po (unstressed)							
	tial spelling of 'shul'							
tremendous	tre (unstressed e)							
	ous ending							
effects	affects/effects confusion							
	double f							
disastrous	er + ous = rous							
	ous ending							
recommend	single c; double mm							
advice	ce/se confusion							
	single d							
preferring	stressed fer							
	double r to add ing							
properties	unstressed e							
	+ es change y to i							
electricity	electric							
	+ ity							
accommodation	double letters							
	ation							
essentials	double ss							
	tial spelling of 'shul'							
possibility	ible							
	ible + ity = ibility							
miraculous	mirac(le)							
	+ ulous							
technology	ch spelling of 'k'							
	root ology							
Total errors per pupil								

Error analysis of independent writing

Name:	
Class:	Date:

Samples: 1. _____

2. _____

Error analysis

Misspelling	Notes/analysis	Misspelling	Notes/analysis

Analysis of strengths and weaknesses

Strengths (strategies and guidelines used **effectively**)	Weaknesses (what needs to be worked on)

Action plan

From: **Spelling: Teacher's Resource Book** by Carol Matchett (ISBN 978 07217 1219 2). Copyright © Schofield & Sims Ltd, 2013. Published by Schofield & Sims Ltd, Dogley Mill, Fenay Bridge, Huddersfield HD8 0NQ, UK (www.schofieldandsims.co.uk). This page may be photocopied after purchase for use within your school or institution only.